messy parables

The Bible Reading Fellowship
15 The Chambers, Vineyard
Abingdon OX14 3FE
brf.org.uk

The Bible Reading Fellowship (BRF) is a Registered Charity (233280)
Messy Church is part of BRF
Messy Church® is a registered word mark
and the logo is a registered device mark of BRF

ISBN 978 0 85746 550 4
First published 2017
Reprinted 2017
10 9 8 7 6 5 4 3 2 1
All rights reserved

Acknowledgements
Unless otherwise stated, scripture quotations are taken from The Holy Bible, New
International Version (Anglicised edition) copyright © 1979, 1984, 2011 by Biblica.
Used by permission of Hodder & Stoughton Publishers, an Hachette UK company.
All rights reserved. 'NIV' is a registered trademark of Biblica. UK trademark number
1448790.

Scripture quotations from the Contemporary English Version. New Testament
© American Bible Society 1991, 1992, 1995. Old Testament © American Bible Society
1995. Anglicisations © British & Foreign Bible Society 1996. Used by permission.

Scripture taken from the Holy Bible, New International Reader's Version®. Copyright
© 1996, 1998 Biblica. All rights reserved throughout the world. Used by permission
of Biblica.

Every effort has been made to trace and contact copyright owners for material used
in this resource. We apologise for any inadvertent omissions or errors, and would
ask those concerned to contact us so that full acknowledgement can be made in
the future.

A catalogue record for this book is available from the British Library

Printed and bound by CPI Group (UK) Ltd, Croydon CR0 4YY

messy parables

25 retellings for all ages

Martyn Payne

BRF

Contents

Introduction

There is no doubt that a well-told story rarely fails to attract and hold an audience. And so it's no surprise that it is the Bible passages that tell a tale that work best when it comes to the Messy Church celebration. Working with a theme or doctrinal truth is always a much more challenging ask of the Messy team and of the Messy storyteller. It is a huge relief and encouragement, therefore, to discover that Jesus, surely the best of communicators, almost always chose stories as the way to captivate his messy audiences.

Stories are every bit as powerful and effective as the best of sermons, however well their teaching is presented. In fact, stories often do a better job, as all speakers will testify when they receive feedback on what was said. It is invariably the story that is remembered long after the bullet points on the screen have been forgotten.

Some of the best Bible stories are, of course, the parables of Jesus, which is why this book is devoted to creative ways of telling them with today's audiences, whether in Messy Church or other multigenerational church settings. Each parable will, I hope, inspire you to become a better Bible storyteller, particularly in Messy Church where so many of these stories have never been heard before. They still have the potential to transform people's lives as they enable families to meet with God in the story, as well as through the storybook people of God who they encounter during two hours of creativity, celebration and a shared meal.

The first part of this book contains some insights and ideas to help you become a storyteller. It explores the power of story, and of parables in particular, as well as the challenge of sharing the story with a pan-generational audience. There is also advice on how to go about creating your own Messy stories. In the second part you will find the parables themselves. When Jesus talked with his disciples about why he used parables, he gave this advice for teachers and by inference for faith storytellers:

> [Jesus] said to them: 'Therefore every teacher of the law who has become a disciple in the kingdom of heaven is like the owner of a house who brings out of his storeroom new treasures as well as old.'
>
> MATTHEW 13:52

This is exactly what Jesus did with his parables. They were very often stories that drew on existing themes in the Jewish scriptures, such as shepherds and sheep, sibling rivalry and the care of vineyards, but to which he then introduced new elements and unexpected twists that made the stories unique and which took his audiences into unexplored territory. They were a captivating mix of the familiar and the unknown.

This collection of creative ways to tell 25 of the parables tries to emulate this pattern for audiences today. I have drawn on tried-and-tested storytelling approaches and familiar formats such as nursery rhyme, simple drama and the use of visual aids, but I have also brought the material up to date with contemporary references and language that will resonate with a Messy Church congregation.

Some of the stories have already appeared in an earlier format on the BRF Children and Families website, but they have been revised and reshaped; the majority are brand new. You could say that this book itself is a mixture of old and new treasures. For each parable there are some background notes, which are designed both to unpack the more obscure references that would have been understood only by audiences at the time, and to help the storyteller think through the story. And the stories themselves use a variety of styles. One of my aims in writing this book has been to introduce leaders to alternative ways of telling Bible stories, which I hope will stretch the users' skills as they have a go at new approaches. I hope that this will nurture and develop your God-given gift of storytelling, as well as help you find your own authentic storytelling voice. Finally, there is a suggested Messy Church congregational prayer activity suitable for all ages that links with the content of the parable and the storytelling. The Bible passages for each parable are taken from the New International Version (NIV) unless otherwise stated.

Jesus used his special stories to challenge his listeners to think again about life and death, about heaven and hell, about themselves and their neighbours, and about the ways of this world and those of the kingdom of heaven. We are invited to do the same for our generation, using the gift of these stories to help new audiences hear and respond to God's call to put their trust in him.

> My people, hear my teaching; listen to the words of my mouth. *I will open my mouth with a parable; I will utter hidden things, things from of old* – things we have heard and known, things our ancestors have told us. We will not hide them from their descendants; *we will tell the next generation the praiseworthy deeds of the Lord, his power, and the wonders he has done.* He decreed statutes for Jacob and established the law in Israel, which he commanded our ancestors to teach their children, *so the next generation would know them, even the children yet to be born, and they in turn would tell their children. Then they would put their trust in God.*
>
> PSALM 78:1–7a (emphasis mine)

Part 1

All about storytelling

The importance of story

Live storytelling is back in fashion… or maybe it never went away.

In a world that seems dominated by multimedia presentations, YouTube videos, DVDs and computer-mediated friendships, the wonderful novelty of face-to-face storytelling is a breath of fresh air, particularly for today's digital generation.

Live Bible storytelling is enjoying a revival too, which of course was always the way it was meant to be. There is no mistaking the importance and power of stories about God, told by storytellers whose hearts have been touched by those very same stories. However, none of this should surprise us. Our Christian Bible is the holy repository of 66 books-worth of stories that were originally alive on people's lips and which were passed on faithfully down the generations. The oral tradition existed long before the written word and it is still part of our DNA. Human beings love to tell stories. Just spend some time watching and listening to people in your local café or on the bus to discover that this is true.

We tell stories to each other to build relationships, to pass on news (and gossip), to make sense of what is happening to us and to wrestle with the big questions of life. Not all of this happens at the same time, of course, or even in the same conversation, but this is the sort of storytelling that makes us tick as communities. It is as we talk through things together that we learn to see the world differently from another's point of view and, as a result, that person's story helps shape and develop our own. One possible translation of John's famous opening verse from the first chapter of his Gospel is, 'In the beginning was the conversation'. We are made in the image of God and part of this likeness is found in the fact that we love to tell stories to each other and be in conversation, just as God is within the Trinity.

And when it comes to trying to get our heads around the ultimate questions about life, death and the universe, people have always turned to stories to make sense of it all. If, for example, you were to ask one of God's people in the Old Testament what their God was like, they definitely wouldn't have replied by listing a series of theological truths about God's nature. Rather, they would have told you their story, their experience of God. 'Well, let me tell you about when we were slaves in Egypt...' they would begin, and so the storytelling would start. You can read one such example of this for yourself in Psalm 105:12–45. And it was exactly this story that was repeated year on year at the Passover festival, when the family gathered around the storytelling table and the youngest child present asked, 'What makes this night so special?'

Stories invite us into a safe, shared space of listening where we can make our own discoveries about how what we hear might impact us today. Whether we are listening to the story of Joseph on his long journey from being an unlovely, boastful brother to when he rescues his whole family from famine, or of Ruth bravely deciding to stay with her mother-in-law and become an outsider in a new land, or of Job wrestling with why the innocent should suffer in this world, we are drawn into the story, inspired by the thoughts and ideas there and moved to find out more about who God is, who we are and who we are meant to become.

Stories can be received on many different levels and what we take from a story often depends on our level of engagement with what we are hearing. So how does that work? Why not try the following fun exercise, which I've often used with groups in storytelling workshops to help them understand the importance and impact of story?

- First take a deep breath and hold that in. This is like the story being taken into us, literally an initial 'in-spiration'.
- Next let out the air with a long 'ahh' sound. This is our time to think about the story, a time to wonder and find ourselves in the story.
- Then lift one finger up as a gesture of discovery and turn the long

'ahh' into an 'ah-ha'. This is that moment when the story begins to make sense and show us something new.

- Finally, lift up both hands with thumbs up on each and a broad smile or even a laugh as you turn the 'ah-ha' into 'ha-ha'. This is that moment of insight from the story that will stay with you for ever. It is a moment of transformation. The story is part of you now and you are part of the story.

This is how the best stories work and, in particular, it is how the stories of God can touch our lives. Our job as storytellers is to allow the Bible story to do its work in this way, both inspiring and transforming people for the better. This is why Jesus told stories as his preferred method for passing on the great truths about God and it is why Christians still do so today. Of course, stories can still be impactful when they come second-hand on a screen, but there is no doubting that something special happens when we hear a story directly from another person, particularly a person who tells that story from the heart because he or she has themselves been transformed by that very story.

It is our privilege and calling in church – whether Messy or otherwise – to let Bible stories do their work in this way, lifting them off the page and allowing them to breathe their blessing into the lives of those who listen. There is an old Chinese proverb that says that 'the shortest distance between a person and a truth is a story'. In other words, stories are the best way in which we can discover truths about the world, ourselves and God. Nathan the prophet understood this when he was asked by God to tell King David that he had committed murder and adultery after he had stolen Bathsheba from her husband Uriah (2 Samuel 12:1–14). A direct accusation of the terrible sin wasn't going to work, so instead Nathan told a story and it was this that touched David most powerfully and awoke his conscience. It was certainly the shortest and most effective way to the truth.

Bible stories do just this: open eyes to God's presence, hearts to God's love and minds to God's truth. So let's get busy telling Bible stories again… live, direct and with passion!

The power of parable

Whenever our BRF team has run workshops on Bible storytelling and we have asked members of the group to name their favourite Bible story, the majority inevitably opt for one of the parables of Jesus: perhaps 'the lost sheep', 'the good Samaritan' or 'the prodigal son'. These famous stories of Jesus have consistently been among the top ten favourites for storytellers and audiences alike since they were first told. Everyone loves a good story, but there are some stories that stay with us way beyond the storytelling. They have a special power to go on working in our hearts and minds long after the story-time session has ended. The parables of Jesus are just such stories.

So what is it that is so special about these short stories drawn from everyday life in first-century Palestine, and why do we still use them today? And why can they still entertain, inspire and challenge audiences in the 21st century with as much power as they once did the farmers and fishermen of Galilee long ago?

When Jesus told parables, he was making use of a long-established tradition in Jewish rabbinical teaching. There are examples of parables in the Old Testament, and the ancient commentaries on the Hebrew Scriptures known as the Midrash often debated the meaning of a text by further storytelling in this style. However, in our western post-enlightenment world, where statements of fact are still largely the accepted way in which truths about life are passed on, it is easy to miss the unique contribution of story to transmit powerful ideas. Storytelling has been the normal way most ancient cultures, and indeed many in the developing world even today, pass on what they feel is precious in their worldview. There will be stories about family, of course, and its traditions, but also those that are about made-up families, and even animal stories, which can carry wisdom for the next generation.

What is unique about this means of passing on insights and information is that it demands that the listener work out the meaning for him- or herself. This is where its true power lies. It isn't about delivering facts to be received (or not), but rather telling stories, within which we discover truths for ourselves. And when we learn something for ourselves, that is more likely to stick and transform our thinking much more profoundly than a simple intellectual assent to someone else's factual proposition.

This is the tradition and the culture within which Jesus moved, and his use of the special stories, which we call parables, was developed in this context in order to help his audience make sense of the startling truths about the kingdom of God. The basic facts about this world are of one order, but to describe what it's like in the kingdom of heaven demands a much greater mental leap and stretch of our imaginations. Only parables could introduce us to spiritual concepts that are radically new and different, where the first become last and the last first, where the poor are the ones who are rich and where children need to lead adults into faith. In order to achieve this, Jesus made use of parables that shocked his listeners into thinking differently; in fact, into having their thinking turned quite inside out and upside down.

Parables are far more than quaint stories about everyday life. Once you start looking at them seriously, you can't help but notice that they are full of impossible and disturbing things, such as: a shepherd who leaves 99 of his best sheep for the sake of one silly one that has wandered off; or a father who is foolish enough to give his lazy and wayward son half the family inheritance well before it was his due; or traditional enemies, who never normally acknowledged each other, ending up helping and being helped on the road to Jericho. When analysed properly, these special stories are both disturbing and counter-cultural for the audiences at the time, unsettling them into considering truths about God and heaven in a way that would never have been heard if those truths had been shared more directly. It's for this very reason, Jesus tells his followers, that everything has to be in parables. However, for those who sincerely want to find out more – for those whose appetites have been stimulated by the parable and who have begun to see something beyond the story – Jesus was prepared to explore the meaning. These parables are designed to make people think. They may start in the world of the familiar but then, by including a disturbing twist, they get people thinking afresh and wanting to find out more.

Matthew tells us that Jesus never spoke to people without using a parable, but that with his disciples in particular he was willing to go further and unpack truths that the parable contained. Not that there was always just one simple truth, but rather layers of new insights that become slowly apparent. In this way, these stories helped people then and can help us today to understand God's way of seeing things. And of course there are parables everywhere in life, like hidden signposts within creation that point to heaven and the Creator. When Jesus saw everyday objects around him and when he observed the everyday activities of his fellow human beings, he saw beyond what was on the surface and, as a consequence, his stories were a way to encounter deep truths about life.

It is quite possible, for example, that Jesus used several of his parables more than once; this is perhaps one of the ways they stuck in the minds of the disciples. Even among the 40 or more Gospel parables we have on record, there are hints that some of these are variations of the same story, such as the two sons on their father's farm and the two sons asked by their father to help with the harvest, or the two versions of the story of the differing amounts of money given to three servants. All these parables are vehicles for discovering spiritual truths and, as such, they have a lot to offer us in the 21st century as we seek to share the good news about Jesus. They are invitational stories that allow the listener to come as close as he or she wants, in their own time, with their own needs. No one is being forced to respond. Instead, the parable gently persuades and can succeed where a more direct challenge might well fail.

For this reason, there is a strong argument for using parables as an evangelistic tool, such as in Messy Church during the celebration. Jesus' parables are ideally suited for our new postmodern audience of listeners who are reluctant, even suspicious, about hearing too much 'God-talk'. And what is more, these stories are brand new to most of them, as they haven't on the whole already come across them at Sunday school or in church. So not only then do we have good stories that will entertain, but they have the added value of being stories that can open up ways into the kingdom of God.

This is the thinking behind this new Messy Church resource, which offers a variety of creative ways to tell a selection of the parables in a tried-and-tested format that can work with the mixed audience of the Messy Church celebration. Each story introduces Jesus to this new audience and introduces the ways of God through the surprising twist in the tale that can entice people into working it all out for themselves. Just enough story, together with just enough space to wonder, can, by the grace of God, produce just enough of a spark of new insight and understanding to light the flame of faith.

The challenge of all-age storytelling

Welcoming all ages and staying all-age for the activities, the celebration and the shared mealtime has been fundamental to the promotion, resourcing and delivery of Messy Church. There is no Sunday school option for the young, nor indeed was it ever intended that there should be a separate group for some adults to experience it all in another space or at a different time. Messy Church has remained unashamedly a fresh expression of multigenerational church, and as such has been increasingly welcomed by many who feel that for too long church has defaulted to worship and learning in silos segregated by age or interest. We need to 'become Christian' together and not as isolated individuals. Each of us, at whatever age, needs the strengths, gifts, inspiration and challenges that can only be released when we all do church together. This Messy Church value of being all-age is premised on the belief that the journey of faith is done better together than apart.

However, staying together for everything has proved a real stumbling block for some, and the pull of traditional church models of separation for discipleship strong. This is something that we in the Messy Church team are always facing and discussing together. And, particularly when it comes to the celebration time, where everyone intentionally gathers to hear the Bible story, the challenge of doing this with noisy toddlers, active children, hard-to-impress teenagers, mobile phone-addicted parents, all alongside a good number from an older, grandparent generation, who value some quiet in order to listen, has proved a bridge too far. It's just not possible, say many, and so for that reason we need to focus on one group rather than all and just hope that the others will pick up something.

If we do this, then this is what happens: the Bible story either becomes child-centred or only a talk for adults, or perhaps a painful mix of both. In this way, some Messy Church celebrations have fallen into the same trap that most all-age family services on a Sunday morning experienced. Either we talk down to the young or we talk over the heads of the many. Sadly, this does happen and I've been to quite a few Messy Churches where it does; and, being honest, I have fallen into the same pitfalls myself at my own Messy Church. So is there a way forward?

This is where all that has already been written about the importance of story and the power of parable in particular come into their own. Yes, the audience we have at a Messy Church is all-age and, indeed, is very broad too in its knowledge (or not) of the Bible, in its experience of church and its willingness to listen. But this is exactly where stories can work, appealing across the generations with many layers of meaning and with many entry points; stories that, if told well, can capture the attention of the most addicted smartphone users.

In this context it is also important to remember that the Bible storytelling in Messy Church is much more than the story in the celebration. It draws the whole experience of the activities and conversations together before the gathered 'story moment', and it continues in many ways verbally and non-verbally afterwards as what has been experienced together becomes part of table-talk at the meal and is taken back home by the families.

All Bible storytelling can face various pitfalls; these include remaining as superficial entertainment, becoming a didactic sermon, including closed questions and formal teaching, or even just being instructional exhortation. These learning styles may have their place in some contexts, but not in Messy Church. For this we need to take as our model Jesus' own storytelling with parables, which raised more questions than answers, where he gave space for people to discover things for themselves, where there was a conversational approach and listeners were surprised by shock contrasts, lively humour and intriguing statements that engaged everyone. Indeed, the first-century disciples picked up on just this as they took his story out to new people and cultures. They were prepared to vary their approach depending on the audience, whether they were Jewish or Gentile, inner-city or rural. We read examples of this in Paul's varied gospel presentations throughout the story of the Acts of the Apostles.

In this way, it is because Messy Church is working largely among those with little or no church background that the story is best told avoiding religious language, just as Jesus used language from everyday situations in his parables. That contrasted strongly with the 'holy talk' of the religious leaders of his day. And also, just like Jesus, the Messy Church storyteller needs to start in the world of the Messy congregation, drawing together all that they have already begun to explore in the activities. The storytelling is not the starting point, but a gathering together of the threads and the clues to the story that have already been shared.

Then, just as with all good storytelling, the story itself needs to be interactive, visual and open-ended, which is in keeping with the overall Messy Church experience. And don't forget the story is not just for the guests but for all on the team too, and so it needs as much preparation and praying about as any other form of presentation in church.

Perhaps the most important piece of advice for telling Messy stories is that the storyteller should be as excited, puzzled and inspired by the story as he or she hopes the listeners will be. If the storyteller is willing to discover, to learn and to be surprised by what is shared, then the audience will be too. The story should be in their hearts, not just on a piece of paper or read from the open pages of a book.

Of course, the story should be faithful to the original, though at the same time it needs to be brought to life by including contemporary references linked to the characters, action and drama of the plot. It is worth reiterating that these Bible stories are very often being heard for the first time by a Messy Church audience and so we need to trust in their God-inspiration to surprise and challenge. They are part of the varied toolbox available for those in Messy Church to help prepare hearts and minds to encounter God for the first time and to discover more about Jesus.

The storytelling moment in Messy Church is a gathered time where the all-age Messy family comes together. It has something of the flavour of the 'speeches moment' at the wedding reception, the singing of 'happy birthday' at the party, or the shared applause at a prize-giving; it's the campfire moment on a camping trip where all are together gathered around the story, each bringing their different experiences of the rest of Messy Church into one. It is not the most important part of Messy Church – thinking that way is a hangover from the days of regarding the sermon or the Eucharist as the true high point of a church gathering – nor is it the 'proper church' moment. It is no more or less important than the other parts of Messy Church, requiring the same amount of attention to detail and the inclusion of hospitality, creativity and being all-age as the rest. The story needs to be wrapped prayerfully in welcome, warmth and wonder to allow it to work. It is simply an opportunity to fit together the pieces of the whole Messy Church story jigsaw for that session and, therefore, should continue in the same style as everything else, before and after, namely being participative, conversational and fun; sharing with people, not talking at them.

In this context, Messy storytelling works best if it draws on what people have already begun to explore, revolves around one key point and involves everyone – don't just talk to children, nor just to the adults; and if you're going to include people actively in the story, make sure you involve people from different generations. Most importantly, Messy Church stories need to be told with passion and commitment from the heart.

The Messy parables in this book will hopefully provide you with some models of how to achieve this but, in the end, no book can substitute for plenty of practice and preparation. The truth is, if you want to communicate with all ages, then you must determine to do just that from the start and be prepared to think all-age about every aspect of the story – the visuals, the anecdotes, the activities, the references and the questions. You will need to check that you are engaging everyone, not just the most active or the noisiest. You will need to use language that works for different age groups and interests, which will probably mean saying the same things more than once but using alternative, relevant words. You will need deliberately to make an effort to include your whole audience in what you are sharing, not just those nearest to you. And you will need to avoid the temptation to talk only with those who respond the best, be that the children or your own team. Jokey asides to one section of the Messy congregation can be very distracting and annoying. Let everything say clearly, 'This story is for everyone!'

Multigenerational storytelling is possible but, to do it well, we need to trust the power of the God-inspired story, trust that the Holy Spirit is at work in our God-loved audience and trust in Jesus to equip you with the gifts you need to tell stories like he did. These are the stories that have changed lives down the centuries and that will continue to do so if we are ready to tell them afresh in our generation.

Becoming a Messy storyteller

Telling stories is something all of us can do; it just takes some practice and a few helpful hints. So let's get going.

When it comes to bringing Bible stories to life, then we must of course start with the original story. However familiar you think you are with a Bible passage, always go back and read it again… and again… and again. There is always something more to discover in the text itself. There is so much written word out there in our world today – in newspapers, books and on social media – that most of us have learned to skim-read at speed and to guess what's coming next. Quick reading like this can be a useful skill in many instances, but don't let this creep into your Bible reading.

It is, however, so tempting to rush the reading stage, especially if you have already handled that famous story from this or that Gospel many times before. The trouble is, we usually miss something this way. So take time to read carefully, slowly and, of course, prayerfully. This may be the same passage you spoke about very recently but that was to a different audience, at a different time and under different circumstances. All scripture is timeless and timely; in other words, the story doesn't change, but how God inspires you by his Spirit to tell the story will depend on the particular audience and setting you have on the day.

As we have already explored above, Messy congregations can be of a very particular sort – mixed, restless maybe, new to this God-talk and certainly unfamiliar with the Christian language and assumptions that you might so easily bring to your storytelling. So before you start, take time to read the passage several times, asking God to show you what resonances this story might have for your listeners, what starting points will make sense, what language will help and what will confuse them, and what the original story is saying today to the families who will be in front of you.

So what next? I have found it helps to explore the passage with a series of useful prompts that will hopefully help you find your best way into telling the story. I have often used the following storytelling grid as a guide in workshops and people have found it useful. It looks like this:

So what does each visual prompt mean? Moving from left to right and top to bottom, here is an explanation:

1 What feelings and emotions are there in the story?
2 What people are there in the story – not only those mentioned by name?
3 What objects are there in the story?
4 What sounds?
5 What still surprises and puzzles you about the story?
6 What tastes are there?
7 And what smells?
8 What would make a good opening line (1), what is the turning point (2) and what will be the final line (3) for your story?
9 What movements are there in the story?

Not all of these ways will work for every storyteller. Some people find that they hear the sounds of the story better than picking up on its emotions; others are quicker to imagine themselves into the story and see all sorts of objects and people present rather than relating initially to the movements in the story. We are all different storytellers and we need to find the way into it that suits us best. However, it is useful to consider all the possibilities that this grid throws up, simply because our audience will be a mixture of types of listeners and learners. For some, the smells and tastes will be more important; for others, it will be the key words, sounds or movements and so on. Most important, though, is your own attitude to the story; this is what matters most. Unless *you* feel that this story is worth telling and that *you* have encountered God again within it, challenging and speaking to *you* through the story, you will never be able to tell it well and your audience will certainly find it hard to want to listen for long. Basically, it means falling in love with the Bible story again and this is fundamental to becoming a good storyteller.

You have the story in your heart and you have discovered a way to tell it, so is that it? Well, not quite. So often we then fall into one of two traps when it comes to the last element in good storytelling. Either we turn the story into a sermon at the end, adding the key points that *we* feel it is saying – which may be a key point for some listeners but most usually it is just what God is saying to us in particular. Or, we give the story an abrupt ending and move swiftly on to the prayers or the meal. There is a middle way that is neither didactic nor reductionist.

Stories need time to sink in, time to do their work. This is especially true of Bible stories. So rather than draw out the moral, as you see it, finish instead with some open-ended questions. These questions may well be your own thoughts and wonderings about the story. Show your audience that the story has made you think and that it has taught you something new about others, yourself and God. You might even invite people to contribute their own responses or perhaps to talk to each other in family groups. If you have used a particular, repeated phrase as part of your storytelling or a simple visual, then return to that as you finish and invite everyone to try and make sense of the story for themselves.

Storytelling is a shared experience of discovery, involving storyteller, audience and story. It is not about attaining some prescribed learning outcome, to use the educational jargon, but about learning alongside and from each other. This can be challenging for some of us in leadership who maybe feel that it is our job to make sure a Bible truth has been heard and learned. The truth or truths are in the story and they may be differently received by individuals in the Messy audience, because people and their needs are different and so too are their places on their own journeys of faith. Good storytelling is about letting go and letting God do his work with the story, as he knows best for everyone who listens. No wonder Jesus, on more than one occasion, says: 'He who has ears to hear, let him hear.' In other words, the ultimate responsibility for discovering something from the story isn't the storyteller's, but that of those in the audience.

To finish, here are a few further practical hints that might help as you prepare to tell the story:

- Try and find a one-word hook or a simple repeated phrase that you can use several times throughout the story to give some rhythm and shape to your retelling.
- Use short sentences – don't let them become over-long and full of subordinate clauses. This is why the stories in part 2 are typeset as they are.
- As you tell the story, work with your audience's imaginations. Help them to step into the story and be there alongside Daniel, Jonah, the disciples, or whoever.
- Always involve adults as well as children in any drama. This story is for everyone.
- Draw out questions as well as answers. Think of telling the story as a dialogue.

- Don't be afraid to share your own amazement or maybe your confusion at what you are sharing. Be a listener to your own story.
- Let go of power by being prepared to leave some things open-ended and unanswered.
- Treat the story with respect, as something precious and special. Remember you are sharing a gift from God with others.

I have already written elsewhere and more extensively on creative Bible storytelling, both in the section on the Messy celebration in *Messy Togetherness* (BRF, 2016) and in *Creative Ways to Tell a Bible Story* (BRF, 2013). So if you would like to explore and develop your gift of storytelling further, then I hope you will find some more inspiration and guidance in these books.

Yes, storytelling is possible for all of us; it just takes some practice and prayer. And the more you tell Bible stories, the more you'll discover your own particular style of storytelling that allows God to be at work through his inspired stories, that will in turn become a blessing to all who listen.

Part 2

Messy parables

Visit **messychurch.org.uk/5504** to download the
illustrations for the parables that follow.

1
Messy baking

The parable of the yeast

Again [Jesus] asked, 'What shall I compare the kingdom of God to? It is like yeast that a woman took and mixed into about sixty pounds of flour until it worked all through the dough.'
LUKE 13:20–21

[Jesus] told them still another parable: 'The kingdom of heaven is like yeast that a woman took and mixed into about sixty pounds of flour until it worked all through the dough.'
    Jesus spoke all these things to the crowd in parables; he did not say anything to them without using a parable.
MATTHEW 13:33–34

Get ready

What a simple domestic parable Jesus gives us, one to which all the women in his audience could relate to. They'd all baked bread in their time, both with and without yeast. And yet what a surprising parable too, with references that would have shocked his first-century audience in a way that we might miss today.

Jesus is describing what things are like when God is king and immediately uses a story with a woman at the centre; that would have been unusual from the start. And she used lots of flour – some 18 supermarket bags-worth – 60 pounds – enough to bake bread for 100 people. What sort of extravagant baking is this? And then this kingdom of God is compared to yeast, which is fermented dough – something that is rotting – and which in Jewish tradition represented a bad influence, even a metaphor for evil. What sort of kingdom parallel is this? It would certainly have made his audience sit up and listen. It is not hard perhaps to imagine a mischievous smile on Jesus' lips as he told this tale.

Jesus is describing an ordinary everyday household activity, but offers it to us as a clue to how God is at work in the world.

Get set

You will need some props: some yeast in a packet; a big fluffy loaf of bread; one bag of flour that you can use to represent the 18 bags of flour that the woman used.

It might be timely too to make links to *The Great British Bake Off* and to some of its well-known catchphrases such as 'avoiding a soggy bottom', 'signature bake' and being crowned 'star baker'.

Go!

So much flour and so little yeast! (*Show the yeast and the bag of flour.*)

It's bread-making time.

Imagine you are a contestant on *The Great British Bake Off*. You want to be star baker. You are planning a showstopper. It's the signature bake round and you are dreading a soggy bottom.

You need your bread to be the best… to rise the highest… to bake the crustiest… to taste the sweetest.

How much flour? How much yeast?

You have some water. You have some sugar. You have some salt. You have the yeast… such a small amount of yeast… for so much flour… 18 bags of flour.

27 kg… 60 pounds… 18 bags.

Surely this tiny amount of yeast can't be enough?

Surely this tiny amount of yeast can't make a difference?

So much flour in this story. Such a small amount of yeast.

But this is the way God works, says Jesus. It's what things are like when God is king in our lives. Such a lot of us and only a small amount of God, but it's enough to change everything.

Such a lot of people and just a small amount of God, but it's enough to transform a community.

Such a lot of world and just a small amount of God, but it's enough to turn everything upside down and inside out.

Jesus told a story to help us know what it's like when God is king. It was about a woman baking bread. Join in with the woman as she takes the flour… such a lot of flour.

Invite everyone to join in, miming the actions of pouring the flour from the bags, adding the water, the salt and the sugar and kneading the dough.

Pours the water… adds the salt… sprinkles the sugar… kneads the dough.

And then she adds the yeast. Such a small amount of yeast for such a lot of flour.

Lots of kneading… kneading… kneading.

Then waiting… waiting… waiting.

And watching… watching… watching.

As it starts rising… rising… rising.

This is like God at work in me, in you, in our family, in our community and in our world. Slowly and secretly, out of sight, but powerfully.

The yeast isn't much, isn't beautiful, isn't smart, but it is enough. Enough to turn so much flour into a big fluffy loaf of bread. No, lots of loaves of bread, enough for as many who need to eat.

Show a big fluffy loaf of bread.

So where has the yeast gone now?

And just how many loaves might it make?

But how is this yeast like the kingdom of God?

What *does* the kingdom of God look like? Maybe it is as small and as surprising as yeast?

And what is the flour in this story… *so much flour*?

Prayer idea

It seems that small things are important in the kingdom of God.

It seems that small things are strong in the kingdom of God.

It seems that small things are powerful in the kingdom of God.

Hold finger and thumb together for the word 'small' and then, using both hands, slowly spread the fingers and thumbs away from each other as something invisible expands in front of you for the word 'big'.

Let us welcome God's kingdom that starts **small** into our lives, so it might grow **big**.

Let us welcome God's kingdom that starts **small** into our families, so it might grow **big**.

Let us welcome God's kingdom that starts **small** into our neighbourhood, so it might grow **big**.

Let us welcome God's kingdom that starts **small** into our country, so it might grow **big**.

Let us welcome God's kingdom that starts **small** into our world, so it might grow **big**.

Just like a **small** amount of yeast makes the whole lump of dough grow **big**.

This is what it can be like in the kingdom of God.

Amen

2
Messy bridesmaids

The parable of the ten young women

The kingdom of heaven will be like ten young women who took their lamps and went out to meet the bridegroom. Five of them were foolish and five were wise. The foolish ones took their lamps but did not take any oil with them. The wise ones, however, took oil in jars along with their lamps. The bridegroom was a long time in coming, and they all became drowsy and fell asleep.

At midnight the cry rang out: 'Here's the bridegroom! Come out to meet him!'

Then all the young women woke up and trimmed their lamps. The foolish ones said to the wise, 'Give us some of your oil; our lamps are going out.'

'No,' they replied, 'there may not be enough for both us and you. Instead, go to those who sell oil and buy some for yourselves.'

But while they were on their way to buy the oil, the bridegroom arrived. The women who were ready went in with him to the wedding banquet. And the door was shut.

Later the others also came. 'Lord, Lord,' they said, 'open the door for us!'

But he replied, 'Truly I tell you, I don't know you.'

Therefore keep watch, because you do not know the day or the hour.

MATTHEW 25:1–13

Get ready

Wedding customs in Jesus' time were different from today. The celebrations lasted up to a week after a year of betrothal; the bride waited for the groom to come and fetch her from her home; and there was a procession to the reception at the bridegroom's home, passing through the streets at night, for which the bride's girlfriends would light the way with oil lamps.

This parable raises intriguing and puzzling questions. For example, Jesus had already described himself as a bridegroom in the Gospel story, so is this about him coming to fetch his bride, or brides (the Greek doesn't actually say they were bridesmaids) – a bride that is his church? And why aren't some prepared? Hadn't they expected a delay? And what does 'being prepared' as a church mean? How do we keep the flame of faith burning? And why won't the wise share their oil with the foolish – that doesn't seem fair. Or why doesn't the groom let them in at the end, even saying he doesn't know them – that sounds harsh. Once again, here is a parable that seems to be a deceptively simple story but which is full of deliberately disturbing twists that made audiences sit up and listen.

The context for this parable is a block of teaching in Matthew's Gospel near the end of Jesus' ministry where the focus is on what will happen at the end of time. The first Christians who read this were living through restless times and this parable would have challenged them to keep looking out for Jesus. Surely this is a challenge we also need to hear in today's world?

Get set

The music from Mendelssohn's 'Wedding March' might be useful on a CD, or the tune for 'Here comes the bride'; some visuals from a wedding – such as a veil, small pieces of wedding cake or a bouquet – will also help set the scene.

Go!

Play the opening bars to Mendelssohn's 'Wedding March' or else start humming 'Here comes the bride'. Encourage everyone to hum along.

Everyone loves a wedding.

Who's been to a wedding recently?

Share some wedding stories with and from the congregation briefly. The wedding props could be used here.

In our part of the world it's the groom who usually waits for the bride to arrive, but in Jesus' day it was the bride who waited for the groom.

Sing, with changed words, 'Here comes the groom'.

And how long have you ever known a groom to be kept waiting for his bride?

In our part of the world the groom has to wait... maybe up to an hour? In Jesus' day the bride might have waited hours and hours until it was late into the evening.

But she would have had her friends around. They were waiting too, to light up the procession back to the groom's home for the reception – once he eventually arrived, that is.

It might have been a long wait.

It would have been dark – no street lights in those days.

It might mean relying on extra supplies of lighter fuel – in those days oil for hand-held lamps.

'Be prepared' is the Scout motto. But some of the bride's friends had clearly not been in the Girl Guides.

Jesus told a story about a wedding; about a bride waiting with ten girlfriends for the bridegroom.

And he was late... and it was dark... and five of them hadn't reckoned on him being delayed.

It was midnight when the cry finally went up, 'He's coming.'

But all the lamps had burned low. They'd all run out of fuel.

Five of the bride's friends had brought some extra, just in case, which was enough for them but not enough for the other five to use as well. These other five had to go off to buy some more.

By the time they had come back, the bridegroom had come… and gone. The procession had started without them. They were at the back of the crowd and so arrived too late for the party. The groom didn't even recognise them when they asked to be let in. They missed out on the reception.

This is what it could be like when God comes as king, said Jesus – so make sure you are ready.

It's like…

… being in the crowd to watch the Tour de France cyclists go by, ready to capture the moment on your phone. But the race is delayed and your battery, which had been low in the first place, runs out. While you dash back to the car to top it up with a charger, the race goes by. You miss out.

It's like…

… waiting to see a famous celebrity by the roadside, but she is delayed. The weather changes and, though your friends have thought to bring along macs and hoods, you are getting drenched. So you dash to the shops nearby for a cheap umbrella. While you're away, she goes by. You miss the moment.

It's like…

… looking forward to being part of the evening carnival procession down by the beach on holiday. You have your Chinese lantern ready with a tea light burning safely inside. But the start is delayed and your tea light runs out. Others have brought a spare one, but not you. And by the time you are back from the guest house with another light, the procession has begun without you and you are left behind.

You've missed your chance.

The coming of God is like this, says Jesus. It might mean waiting sometimes. It may be delayed but then suddenly God is there. Will you be ready?

Ready to hear God's voice when he speaks to you?

Ready to say 'yes' to God when he calls?

Ready to join in with his plans when he arrives?

Or will you, like five of the young women in the parable, be unprepared? Be busy doing something else? Or maybe not expecting God to show up at all?

Don't miss out on the party of love God has prepared for you.

Prayer idea

Make a fist of one hand with the thumb just sticking up a little so it looks like a lamp with its wick showing.

Here is the lamp the young women had. Will it be alight when God comes, or will it have run out of oil?

Help us, Lord God, to keep the light of our faith in you burning bright as we…

Pray to you – **hands into a prayer position.**
Read the Bible – **two open palms like an open book.**
Listen to your Holy Spirit – **hands by ears.**
Love you, our neighbour and ourselves – **create a heart shape with the index finger and thumb from both hands.**
Help us to live with our faith burning bright this week – **make a fist again of one hand with the thumb sticking out a little but moving slightly like a flickering flame.**
Amen

3
Messy brothers

The parable of the two sons

[Jesus said,] 'What do you think? There was a man who had two sons. He went to the first and said, "Son, go and work today in the vineyard."

'"I will not," he answered, but later he changed his mind and went.

'Then the father went to the other son and said the same thing. He answered, "I will, sir," but he did not go.

'Which of the two did what his father wanted?'

'The first,' they answered.

Jesus said to them, 'Truly I tell you, the tax collectors and the prostitutes are entering the kingdom of God ahead of you. For John came to you to show you the way of righteousness, and you did not believe him, but the tax collectors and the prostitutes did. And even after you saw this, you did not repent and believe him.'

MATTHEW 21:28–32

Get ready

This is one of Jesus' final parables told during Holy Week. His authority is being challenged by the religious leaders, particularly after his noisy entry into Jerusalem on a donkey and then the business with the money changers in the Temple. Jesus seems to be more on the offensive in these exchanges, perhaps because he knows his time is short and he is longing for the leaders to change their minds. This parable is so simple but profound and would surely have stuck in the minds of his audience. Might they be ready, like the first son, to rethink their opinions about John the Baptist and, therefore, about Jesus too?

This harvest story of family life would be easily recognisable to those from the agrarian society of Jesus' day. Who hadn't experienced children who said they would help with the harvest but then didn't? But maybe surprises do happen. They might say 'no' initially but then change their mind. It's actions that matter in the end, not words.

This story about two sons has echoes of the parable of the prodigal son. In that too, there was one son who was awkward and rebellious but who eventually changed his mind (repented), and another son who seemed loyal and industrious but was secretly harbouring discontent. Both parables would have shocked those who thought themselves to be God's faithful people. There is a powerful sting in the tail of this harvest story, where Jesus says that it is the unlikely – the outcasts on the edges of society – who will be welcomed into heaven before the religious experts.

Get set

This is a harvest story about a vineyard. The retelling below uses a more familiar setting for those of us in the UK of an orchard and apple trees. You will need a big rosy red apple as a visual, as well as a basket containing a number of the same type of apples and one similar apple cut in half to reveal its heart-shape cross section.

N.B. There are a number of apple-related puns and references in the story that you may or may not want to draw attention to.

Go!

Show a rosy red apple and engage the congregation with some conversation about apples.

This apple looks juicy and tasty. Or maybe you prefer green apples? Perhaps you have your own apple tree in your garden? Or you've been apple-picking some time? And how do you eat your apple? Slowly, bite by bite; even swallowing the core? Or do you core it first… and peel it?

Today's story is about apples… well, actually, when Jesus first told the story, it was about grapes… but it works just as well with apples.

This apple story concerns one Mr Smith. He is a fruit farmer and owns an orchard where, among other things, he grows apples. Now, Mr Smith comes from a long line of fruit farmers. His mother's mother was one of the great apple-growers of her day. She was the original Granny Smith.

Well, Mr Smith was inspecting his orchard one day. The apples were nice and red and juicy. And as he walked by one tree… plonk… one fell right on his head. Mr Smith immediately realised the gravity of the situation. It was time for harvest. He picked up the apple. 'Cor!' he said, 'It's picking time. I'd better go and get some help.'

Now back at the farm, known as Bramley Manor, were Mr Smith's two sons. They were the apple of their parents' eyes. Two fine young lads. Their names were Noel and Wilbut.

Mr Smith needed their help with the harvest, so he went to Noel first to *ap-peal* for his assistance. 'Noel, my boy, I need your help to pick the apples. Will you come?'

'No,' said Noel. 'Can't you see I'm busy right now?' Dad went off, very disappointed.

But in fact, a little while later, Noel was sorry for not being helpful, so he changed his mind. He picked up a basket and set off to the orchard to help his dad after all.

Now, you will remember that Mr Smith has two sons, so in the meantime he had gone off to find Wilbut. 'Wilbut, my boy, I need your help to pick the apples. Will you come?'

'But of course, Dad,' Wilbut replied. 'I'll come and help. I won't be a moment. I'll just change into my old jeans.'

Meanwhile, in the orchard, Noel, who had changed his mind, had now joined his dad, pipping his brother to the post. He was soon up a ladder, taking great care to pick the apples carefully so they wouldn't drop and get bruised. Very soon, his first basket was full.

'Well done, son,' laughed Mr Smith. He was really pleased with Noel. 'Here are some more baskets. We'll get this done in *juice* no time at all!'

Produce the full basket of apples.

But what about Wilbut? There was no sign of him. What about his promise to come and help? Surely he couldn't still be changing into his old jeans?

Yes, you've guessed it.

Wilbut was still sitting in the chair where his dad first found him. He'd even dozed off to sleep.

Now, who do you think pleased Mr Smith the most? Noel or Wilbut?

Ask your audience and hear their reasons why.

Jesus is talking about two sorts of people.

There are those like Noel, who say '*No*' and then '*Well…* OK!'

And those like Wilbut, who initially say they *will, but* then do nothing.

Maybe the dad in this story, as so often in Jesus' parables, is like God, and the sons are you and me.

We may have said 'no' to God but there is always the chance to change our mind. Worse, though, is to say 'yes' but then do nothing about it.

I wonder whether you are a Noel or a Wilbut when it comes to God?

Prayer idea

Show the single red apple again.

Maybe we can use an apple to help us pray.

If you cut one open, look at the shape of its cross-section. It is a heart.

Show the apple you have cut in two.

Jesus talked elsewhere about people who say 'yes' with their lips but whose hearts are far from God.

Invite everyone to touch either their lips or their heart as you share the following prayer:

> Forgive us, Lord Jesus, that we have often been too quick to say things with our *lips* that we did not mean in our *hearts*.
>
> Thank you that we can always change our mind and come home to you even if we have said 'no' with our *lips* but now want to say 'yes' in our *hearts*.
>
> Help us, Lord Jesus, to love you with our *hearts* as well as our *lips*.
>
> Help us Lord Jesus, to say 'yes' to following you with our *hearts* this coming week, not just with our *lips*.
>
> Amen

4
Messy builders

The parable of the wise and foolish builders

[Jesus said,] 'Therefore everyone who hears these words of mine and puts them into practice is like a wise man who built his house on the rock. The rain came down, the streams rose, and the winds blew and beat against that house; yet it did not fall, because it had its foundation on the rock. But everyone who hears these words of mine and does not put them into practice is like a foolish man who built his house on sand. The rain came down, the streams rose, and the winds blew and beat against that house, and it fell with a great crash.'

MATTHEW 7:24–27

[Jesus said,] 'As for everyone who comes to me and hears my words and puts them into practice, I will show you what they are like. They are like a man building a house, who dug down deep and laid the foundation on rock. When a flood came, the torrent struck that house but could not shake it, because it was well built. But the one who hears my words and does not put them into practice is like a man who built a house on the ground without a foundation. The moment the torrent struck that house, it collapsed and its destruction was complete.'

LUKE 6:47–49

Get ready

This well-loved parable comes after a block of teaching in both Matthew's and Luke's Gospels. On both occasions it underlines a key element from all that Jesus has said, namely that hearing his words is not enough; people need to put them into practice. At the end of the chapters in Matthew that we call 'The Sermon on the Mount', it joins other powerful illustrations that urge his listeners to find the narrow path, to become the healthy tree that bears fruit and not simply to use the right words while failing to do what God says.

The contrast between the wise and foolish man must have made his hearers think about many similar verses in the book of Proverbs (for example, Proverbs 12:15). Hearing in the Bible is about far more than just acknowledging a voice; it is about taking advice to heart and acting on it.

The two versions of this parable each add some extra detail to the other, in particular Luke's words that 'he dug down deep' and Matthew's that the second man 'built on sand'. These two images have stood the test of time when used to describe the seriousness of a person's commitment to a cause or, in this case, the reality of someone's Christian discipleship.

Shoddy housebuilding by 'cowboy builders' would have been something that Jesus' audience understood well. Once again, he is using ideas that make ready sense. And also, given that storms in Palestine tended to be very sudden, with a lot of rain falling in a short space of time, the violent crash and complete destruction described at the end of the parable is not an exaggeration either.

Get set

You will need some children's wooden building blocks of varying sizes to use in the introduction.

The parable retelling makes use of the nursery rhyme tune for 'This is the way...' which you may dare to sing, encouraging everyone to join in with you.

Go!

If you have a box Bible, such as is suggested in Creative Ways to Tell a Bible Story *(BRF, 2013, p. 28), you could use this with the wooden blocks rattling mysteriously inside to introduce this parable. If not, just produce the blocks and tumble them out onto a flat surface where everyone can easily see them.*

I wonder what I can do with these?

Take some suggestions, which hopefully will include building various things. Try and build to order but deliberately do it in an unsafe way by putting big blocks on top of small blocks and small blocks as a foundation. Watch it all topple each time with growing dismay and amusement.

What's wrong?

Take the suggestion of using bigger blocks as a strong base or foundation. Build a tower that stands in this way.

Of course, buildings need a strong foundation. But it's not just buildings that work best this way. Maybe our plans, our projects and even our lives need strong foundations too?

Jesus told a building story once. But I don't think it was really about building.

Listen and decide what you think. There were two builders – Mr Wise and Mr Foolish.

Join in as soon as you have picked up the words and actions for each verse.

1 *(action – digging deeply)*
This is the way a wise man builds,
wise man builds, wise man builds.
This is the way a wise man builds,
He digs down deep.

2 *(action – mixing the concrete)*
This is the way a wise man builds,
wise man builds, wise man builds.
This is the way a wise man builds,
He builds on rock.

3 *(action – slowly lifting block on to block)*
This is the way a wise man builds,
wise man builds, wise man builds.
This is the way a wise man builds,
He takes his time.

4 *(action – hammering, sawing and wiping the sweat from his brow)*
This is the way a wise man builds,
wise man builds, wise man builds.
This is the way a wise man builds
 Till the build is done.

5 *(action – throwing building materials and sand into the air randomly)*
This is the way a foolish man builds,
foolish man builds, foolish man builds.
This is the way a foolish man builds,
He builds on sand.

6 *(action – quick building actions with fist on fist)*
This is the way a foolish man builds,
foolish man builds, foolish man builds.
This is the way a foolish man builds,
He builds it quick.

7 *(action – leaning back with hands behind head relaxing)*
This is the way a foolish man builds,
foolish man builds, foolish man builds.
This is the way a foolish man builds,
He finishes first.

Pause song.

But… the rain started to fall.

Invite everyone to tap with one finger on the palm of the hand; then with two fingers, three and so on. It will sound like a rainstorm growing stronger and stronger.

8 *(action – a big clap at the end)*
The house on the sand didn't last long,
didn't last long, didn't last long.
The house on the sand didn't last long.
It fell with a crash.

9 *(action – strong man action on the last line)*
The house on the rock stayed upright and strong,
upright and strong, upright and strong.
The house on the rock stayed upright and strong.
It survived the storm.

Rock was a good foundation for the wise man's house, wasn't it?

So what might be a good foundation for us if we want to stay upright and strong? What good advice should we listen to? What, according to Jesus, makes a good foundation for life?

But will we listen? And will we put it into practice?

Prayer idea

The response for the following short prayers is: 'Help me to do what Jesus says' with palms opened like an open book, which is where we can find the words of Jesus. Teach this response.

Lord God, when I don't know which way to turn this week.
Help me to do what Jesus says.

Lord God, when I feel tempted to act foolishly this week.
Help me to do what Jesus says.

Lord God, when others need my help this week, even though I'm tired.
Help me to do what Jesus says.

Lord God, when I see things that are unfair this week.
Help me to do what Jesus says.

Amen

5
Messy choices

The parable of the rich man and Lazarus

[Jesus continued,] 'There was a rich man who was dressed in purple and fine linen and lived in luxury every day. At his gate was laid a beggar named Lazarus, covered with sores and longing to eat what fell from the rich man's table. Even the dogs came and licked his sores.

'The time came when the beggar died and the angels carried him to Abraham's side. The rich man also died and was buried. In Hades, where he was in torment, he looked up and saw Abraham far away, with Lazarus by his side. So he called to him, "Father Abraham, have pity on me and send Lazarus to dip the tip of his finger in water and cool my tongue, because I am in agony in this fire."

'But Abraham replied, "Son, remember that in your lifetime you received your good things, while Lazarus received bad things, but now he is comforted here and you are in agony. And besides all this, between us and you a great chasm has been set in place, so that those who want to go from here to you cannot, nor can anyone cross over from there to us."

'He answered, "Then I beg you, Father, send Lazarus to my family, for I have five brothers. Let him warn them, so that they will not also come to this place of torment."

'Abraham replied, "They have Moses and the Prophets; let them listen to them."

'"No, Father Abraham," he said, "but if someone from the dead goes to them, they will repent."

'He said to him, "If they do not listen to Moses and the Prophets, they will not be convinced even if someone rises from the dead."'

LUKE 16:19–31

Get ready

This parable of Jesus uses dramatic and memorable imagery to make its point and is one of only two parables (the other being that of the sheep and the goats) to take us into the afterlife. In fact, it was a well-known tale in its time, very popular among Jewish storytellers, who liked to speculate on the great reversal that death might bring. Usually these tales had as their main characters a tax collector and a scholar, where the former gets his comeuppance after he dies and the poor-but-noble scholar is honoured at last. However, Jesus, as usual, surprises his audience by retelling it with a rich man, who in Jewish eyes was surely 'blessed by God', and a wretched beggar on the streets, who was obviously not. And he prepares us for this shock reversal when even on this side of death he gives a name to the beggar (such people were traditionally nameless). The name 'Lazarus' means 'God is my help'.

Once again, the kingdom of God turns our ideas inside out and upside down; some things that may not always be obvious in this life are in this parable revealed after death. However, this parable is not about what it will be like when we die – Jesus is merely making use of the colourful imagery available in his day – but it is about how we use our wealth. In this respect, it picks up on the teaching arising from the previous parable in Luke about a dishonest manager (see Luke 16:9). The love of money leads to all sorts of selfishness, which the law and prophets clearly challenged (for example, see Isaiah 58:6–7) and this is the sin that the rich man in the parable had fallen into. It is also important to note that he takes this same selfishness into death with him, where he still treats Lazarus as his servant and not his equal before God. The great chasm that Abraham talks about is of the rich man's own making and it was forged during his earthly life.

Finally, there is the intriguing reference at the end to whether a man coming back from the dead would make any difference to people like the rich man (in this case, his five brothers). The parable makes it quite clear that it is our decisions and actions in this life that matter and, though such a miracle might amaze people, it is responding to the clear truths of scripture that changes hearts. Of course, Jesus did come back from the dead, but that was to show the world that the great chasm had been bridged; it wasn't a miracle for its own sake.

This unique parable (it occurs in Luke's Gospel as part of a series only he records) touches on a whole raft of questions asked by contemporary audiences. Is this life all there is? Does what we do in this life matter? How do we find our way to heaven? What is important to God? Does God care about those who suffer? Might we create our own hell by our attitudes to others? There is a lot to work with here.

Get set

You will need to prepare two big visuals to represent the protagonists in this parable: a large weighted money bag with a pound sign on one side and a heart on the other; a bundle of rags, which must have been what Lazarus looked like at the rich man's gate, but with a heart hidden among them.

Go!

Place the money bag (pound sign to the front) and the bundle of rags with the heart hidden, on either side of you.

Things aren't always what they seem.

Point to the money bag.

Surely having wealth, riches, lots of money and all the luxury that we can buy is what we all want? It's a good thing.

Well, maybe.

Point to the bundle of rags.

Surely having nothing, being poor, hungry and unloved is not what we want. It's a bad thing.

Well, of course. But is it as simple as that?

We see only what is obvious. God sees the whole picture.

Turn the money bag round to reveal the heart on the other side. Pause and then bring out the heart from among the rags.

God looks beyond the outward appearance. God looks at the heart.

Jesus once told a story about all this.

Pick up either the money bag or the rags, depending on who is being talked about as you tell the following version of the story.

Once there was Mr Rich… and Poor Lazarus.

In fact, Mr Rich was more than rich. He was mega-rich. He lived in total luxury. He had the finest feasts, the finest food, and the finest furnishings.

And Poor Lazarus was more than poor. He was mega-poor. He lived in total squalor: on the streets, living off scraps from the rubbish dump and he was covered in sores. He had only stray dogs for company.

Now, Poor Lazarus used to sit at the gates of Mr Rich's millionaire mansion hoping for a handout, but it never came. As far as Mr Rich was concerned, Poor Lazarus was a nobody – not worth noticing and certainly not worth caring about.

This happens. There are rich people and poor people. It's the way of the world. It will never change, so why try to do anything about it? That's exactly what Mr Rich thought, too.

Then, said Jesus, on the very same day, both men popped their clogs, kicked the bucket, passed away… they both died.

Now, Poor Lazarus went straight to heaven and was welcomed at the great party in the sky. Here he felt clean for the first time, had decent clothes and was loved. It was a bit of a surprise, really, because what good had he ever done?

But Mr Rich went straight to the other place, where there was no welcome, he felt alone and it was unbearably hot. He found that a bit of surprise, to be honest, because after all, what bad had he ever done?

Mr Rich looked from down below to Poor Lazarus up above. 'Help me, please. Help.' In fact, he begged for help just as once Poor Lazarus used to beg Mr Rich for help in his life on earth. But there was nothing that Poor Lazarus could do. There was a huge gap between them both, over which nothing could pass.

Mr Rich called out again, this time to Abraham, God's friend. 'Please send Poor Lazarus to warn my family about this terrible place so they will change their minds. If Poor Lazarus comes back to life, they will think again.'

'No, they won't,' came the reply. 'Even that wouldn't work. They know what to do, just as you knew. It was there all the time in the Bible.' And Mr Rich knew that that was true. He had known what to do but he hadn't done it. Perhaps it wasn't such a surprise, after all.

Jesus finished the story and the crowd went quiet.

What does this mean? What should we do about it? How should we live now? What should we do differently?

Take the money bag again in one hand and the rags in the other.

And what should we do with our money?

And what can we do to help those in need?

And what should we do with our lives?

Prayer idea

The following simple prayer is based on words from John Wesley, who once urged people to 'do all the good you can, by all the means you can, in all the ways you can, in all the places you can, at all the times you can, to all the people you can, as long as ever you can'.

Perhaps you can use the rags and the bag of money to focus everyone's attention on a particular situation of need in the world at this time and what they might do about it.

> Lord God, help us:
> to gain all we can fairly
> to save all we can wisely
> to give all we can generously
> For the sake of your kingdom.
> Amen

6
Messy coins

The parable of the lost coin

[Jesus said,] 'Suppose a woman has ten silver coins and loses one. Doesn't she light a lamp, sweep the house and search carefully until she finds it? And when she finds it, she calls her friends and neighbours together and says, "Rejoice with me; I have found my lost coin." In the same way, I tell you, there is rejoicing in the presence of the angels of God over one sinner who repents.'

LUKE 15:8–10

Get ready

In the central chapters (13—16) of Luke's Gospel, there is a series of stories – most of them unique to Luke – that explore how inclusive and generous God's love is. This was something that would have shocked many religious people of his day. Famous among these stories are the lost-and-found parables including that of the lost coin.

Luke 15:1–3 is the context for this parable and the other lost and found stories. The Message version of the Bible puts it like this: 'By this time a lot of men and women of doubtful reputation were hanging around Jesus, listening intently. The Pharisees and religion scholars were not pleased, not at all pleased. They growled, "He takes in sinners and eats meals with them, treating them like old friends." Their grumbling triggered this story.'

At this stage of his ministry, people were beginning to be either for Jesus or against him. Increasingly, those for him are the outsiders, the marginalised, those who have messy lives and who hang on to his stories, wanting to be close to him. The leaders – the ones who know their scriptures – can't get their heads around this. Jesus is behaving wrongly. He seems to be careless about people's morals. He doesn't seem to appreciate how sinful these other people are. They simply can't quite get the generosity of God.

The ten coins would have formed part of a decorative and valuable headband worn by the woman in the parable. Each silver coin would have been a day's wages. In today's money, an average daily income in the UK is about £60 (after tax).

Each of the lost-and-found stories tries to open up a new understanding about who God is and who we are. None of the stories alone gives the whole picture, but together they paint an amazing portrait of God. It's also typical of Luke to have a balance in his stories between the different sorts of people who lose things and the different sorts of things that are lost, which means that everyone can relate to the stories in some way. The fact that in this parable Jesus chose a woman to represent God would have once again surprised and shocked most of his audience.

Get set

You will need: a box of Liquorice Allsorts; bags, each containing ten 5p coins – one bag per 'family' group of four or five in your Messy congregation. However, before the celebration, remove one of the 5p coins from each of the bags and hide them nearby so that each bag has only nine coins to start with.

Go!

Hand round a plate or a box of Liquorice Allsorts.

Liquorice Allsorts can divide people – some people just hate them, while some love them.

Have a show of hands – for and against.

The very name of these sweets is a way of connecting with what today's parable is about, because 'all sorts' were now coming to Jesus, and some people didn't like it.

Today's parable involves money.

Hand out the bags with the coins to 'family groups'.

How much have you got in each bag?

But for this story there should be ten coins. One of the coins is missing!

Let's tell this parable of Jesus together.

Each time a new part of the story is introduced, each group should move its nine coins around to create outlines of the objects or people mentioned in the story.

Suppose a woman… – can you make the letter W with your nine coins?

Suppose a woman has ten silver coins and loses one… – can you make an outline of a person (arms, legs, head, body) with the nine coins?

The missing coin comes from her precious and valuable headband… – can you make the outline of a headband with one coin obviously missing?

She searched with a lamp… – can you make the outline of a lamp with the nine coins?

And she swept the house… – can you make the shape of a broom with the nine coins?

She searched and searched… – can you make a face with two eyes looking one way and then the other?

She must have been very anxious… – can you make a face with eyes and no smile?

She searched carefully until she found the coin.

Ask each 'family group' to send one person off to find one missing coin.

Now every group should have ten coins.

And when she found it, she was happy… – can you make the outline of a face with a smile, using all ten coins?

She calls her friends and neighbours together and says, 'Be joyful with me; I found my lost coin'… – can you make a line of three friends holding hands from the ten coins?

Can you make a picture of the biggest smile ever with ten coins?

This is the joy of heaven when what is lost is found.

I wonder what heaven will be like… – can you make an outline picture of the beauty and joy of heaven with the ten coins?

Which part of the story do you find most surprising?

Which part of the story do you find puzzling?

Why do you think Jesus chose to tell this particular lost-and-found story?

What might the religious leaders have made of this story?

What is this story saying to us about God?

What is this story saying to us about Jesus?

What is this story saying about us? And about you?

Is this perhaps a story of God searching with all his heart for you and me – a God who shows extravagant love, unstoppable generosity and a relentless unwillingness to give up on us?

Prayer idea

Some people end up lost by mistake, some lose themselves deliberately, but for many, like the coin, it's just an accident and they maybe don't even know they are lost in the first place. God comes searching for everyone because he loves us.

Hand out the Liquorice Allsorts so that everyone has one for the prayer that follows. They can either eat it on the 'amen' or pass it to a friend.

Lord God, thank you for searching for all sorts.
Lord God, thank you for bothering about all sorts, however small and unimportant they might feel.
Lord God, thank you for bothering about me and searching for me so I can experience your love.
Amen

7
Messy contracts

The parable of the workers in the vineyard

[Jesus said,] 'The kingdom of heaven is like a landowner who went out early in the morning to hire workers for his vineyard. He agreed to pay them a denarius for the day and sent them into his vineyard.

'About nine in the morning he went out and saw others standing in the marketplace doing nothing. He told them, "You also go and work in my vineyard, and I will pay you whatever is right." So they went.

'He went out again about noon and about three in the afternoon and did the same thing. About five in the afternoon he went out and found still others standing around. He asked them, "Why have you been standing here all day long doing nothing?"

'"Because no one has hired us," they answered.

'He said to them, "You also go and work in my vineyard."

'When evening came, the owner of the vineyard said to his foreman, "Call the workers and pay them their wages, beginning with the last ones hired and going on to the first."

'The workers who were hired about five in the afternoon came and each received a denarius. So when those came who were hired first, they expected to receive more. But each one of them also received a denarius. When they received it, they began to grumble against the landowner. "These who were hired last worked only one hour," they said, "and you have made them equal to us who have borne the burden of the work and the heat of the day."

'But he answered one of them, "I am not being unfair to you, friend. Didn't you agree to work for a denarius? Take your pay and go. I want to give the one who was hired last the same as I gave you. Don't I have the right to do what I want with my own money? Or are you envious because I am generous?"

'So the last will be first, and the first will be last.'

MATTHEW 20:1–16

Get ready

One of the most often repeated sayings of Jesus is, 'The first shall be last and the last shall be first'. This is a massive challenge to the way things usually work in this world, but the truth is that the kingdom of God turns everything upside down. During his ministry, Jesus regularly demonstrated what this paradox might look like in the way he showed God's love to the social outcast, the unloved stranger and even the hated enemy. This striking parable of the workers in the vineyard tackles head-on the issue of who is first and who is last in God's sight. It echoes the words in Mary's song before Jesus was born when she sang, 'He has brought down rulers from their thrones but has lifted up the humble' (Luke 1:52).

Like so many other parables, this one has the twist in the tale that challenges us to stop and listen, simply because it sounds so unfair. Jesus was brilliant at telling stories that his audience wouldn't easily forget. This story can still upset people today and is guaranteed to get people talking. It is interesting to note that the employer deliberately pays the latecomers first to underline his decision to be equally generous to those who had worked one hour as to those who had toiled for a whole day. This is not a parable about an effective wage incentive policy, but a window into the unlimited grace of God to all.

This parable comes as one response to the conversation Jesus has just had with his followers at the end of the previous chapter about giving up everything for the sake of the kingdom. It can still speak to us today. God's gifts are all through grace; no one earns a heavenly reward. Also, Jesus' audience at the time would have recognised that the vineyard owner was like God. Israel is often described as God's vineyard in the Bible.

The casual labour market was a common sight in first-century Palestine, as not everyone could afford land of their own. The workers waiting for a job would have been poor and the employer in the parable is clearly acting out of compassion and generosity when he chooses to pay them all the same day's wage.

Get set

You will need: lots of 10p pieces and a carton of grapes.

Go!

Ever heard this said before? 'It's just not fair!'

Most of us have a strong sense of what we think is right or wrong, and are particularly upset at any hint of unfairness. We are quick to cry, 'It's not fair!'

Invite everyone to think about any unfair situations they know of and call these out in a sentence that begins 'I think it's unfair that...'

Here's one to get the ball rolling: 'I think it's unfair that footballers get paid more than nurses.'

Encourage lots of responses from all ages.

Today's story from Jesus is about some people who ended up saying: 'It's not fair!'

Next, as another way into the parable, explain that after the story, you are going to serve people according to where each ends up in a queue. Ask everyone to form a queue. After the scuffle has died down and there is an orderly queue, surprise everyone by asking them all to turn around and face the opposite way, so the back of the queue becomes the front.

In today's parable, the big surprise was that the first became last and the last first.

To retell this parable, use some simple playacting, involving the five groups of workers who were hired. Ask for five 'family groups' that include adults and children. All five groups should be invited to lounge on the ground or in their seats waiting for work. Have some 10p pieces ready for the 'silver coins', which were the day's wage.

Today's parable of Jesus is about a man who owned a vineyard. It was harvest time and he needed workers to pick his grapes.

He went to the town square, which was like the local job centre, to find workers.

Go to the first group and employ them, promising a silver coin for their day's work. The group should stand and start to mime picking grapes.

After three hours he went to the market square again and found some more workers to harvest his crop.

Set off the second group picking grapes, promising them a fair wage.

After another three hours, he went to the market square again and found some more workers to help.

Set off the third group picking grapes, promising them a fair wage.

After another three hours, he went to the market square a fourth time and found some more workers to join the harvesters.

Set off the fourth group picking grapes, promising them a fair wage.

After another two hours, he returned to the market square again. There was only one hour of work-time left; nevertheless he found another group and employed them.

Set off the fifth group picking grapes, promising them a fair wage.

The final hour was soon up. It was time to stop. It was pay time.

The first group had been picking grapes for the longest but instead the owner started by giving a silver coin to those in the last group, who had only worked one hour.

Hand out a 10p coin to everyone in the fifth group.

That led the others, and especially those in the first group, to expect more.

Encourage some comment from the groups. Now give 10p coins to each of those in the other four groups.

Invite comments.

Finally give the response of the owner to this unfairness, namely:

The owner said: 'It's what you agreed to. It was the contract. Why shouldn't I be generous with my money, if I want to be?'

What a strange story. Today, the vineyard owner would probably get in trouble with the unions for treating his workers unfairly, or with his boss for managing the business foolishly. In human terms, he is behaving very oddly.

So…

Was it unfair that the first group got what they agreed to?

How was it unfair to the last group? But how is that unfairness different?

Is there a danger of thinking that heaven is a 'first come, first served' sort of place?

What does this parable say heaven is like?

Why might that upset some people?

What is this parable saying about God?

Do you think that maybe the disciples, who were listening, had begun to think that they were 'the first' and that therefore they deserved more from God?

What does this say about God's love for the world?

What is this parable saying to you and me, right now?

Prayer idea

Cut up the grapes into lots of small bunches.

Heaven isn't about first and last; God's love is for everyone equally. This was the scandal of this story at the time and it still makes us think.

Hand out bunches of grapes to groups so that everyone gets a grape. But ask that the first people to receive them must not eat them until everyone, including the very last person, has received a grape.

God is so generous that he wants everyone to experience his love, however long or short a time they have had to wait; however long they have known about God; or however far away from God they have gone.

As everyone enjoys the grapes together in silence, ask them to think about and pray for those people they know who may consider that they are 'last' (perhaps because of unemployment, loneliness, illness or some other sadness). Finish with these words:

> Thank you, Father God, that with you the last can always come first.
> Thank you that Jesus called himself the first and the last.
> Thank you, Father God, that you promise to be with the first and with the last.
> Amen

8
Messy excuses

The parable of the great banquet

He said to him, 'Blessed is the one who will eat at the feast in the kingdom of God.'

Jesus replied: 'A certain man was preparing a great banquet and invited many guests. At the time of the banquet he sent his servant to tell those who had been invited, "Come, for everything is now ready."

'But they all began to make excuses. The first said, "I have just bought a field, and I must go and see it. Please excuse me."

'Another said, "I have just bought five yoke of oxen, and I'm on my way to try them out. Please excuse me."

'Still another said, "I just got married, so I can't come."

'The servant came back and reported this to his master. Then the owner of the house became angry and ordered his servant, "Go out quickly into the streets and alleys of the town and bring in the poor, the crippled, the blind and the lame."

'"Sir," the servant said, "what you ordered has been done, but there is still room."

'Then the master told his servant, "Go out to the roads and country lanes and compel them to come in, so that my house will be full. I tell you, not one of those who were invited will get a taste of my banquet."'

LUKE 14:15–24

Get ready

Jesus is eating again! So much of his teaching in the Gospels came during conversations at a meal table – no wonder the meal is such an important part of the whole experience of worship at Messy Church. This time, Jesus was dining at the home of one of the Pharisees and before he tells this parable he had commented both on the way the guests had all wanted to sit near the host and also on what God's guest list looks like for the party in heaven. This prompted the comment that led to this story.

Those listening to Jesus' story had all accepted invites to the Pharisee's party, but what about the most important invitation of all – God's invitation to be in heaven with him, the greatest party ever? The invited guests in the parable had said they could come, but when it came to the time to turn up they all decided they had other priorities. Jesus was clearly directing his story at the Pharisees and other religious leaders who, by inference, had said 'yes' to God with their lips but when it came to it, put their own interests first. This is, however, also a challenge to all of us. As was obvious from the response to Jesus' ministry, it was the 'poor, crippled, blind and lame' – the nobodies of society, then – who were the willing and welcomed guests at heaven's banquet.

As with all the parables of Jesus, this story would have unsettled his audience with the twist in the tale. The usual A-list celebs didn't bother to turn up, but the unexpected and undeserving crowds who never got invited to anything end up enjoying the feast. Jesus was turning upside down their ideas – and ours – of what God and heaven are like. Heaven is like a party and God's love is much bigger and more open-armed than they could ever have imagined. Are we ready to be surprised by God's love and by who we will meet in heaven?

A similar story is also found in Matthew 22:1–10, where it is a king hosting a wedding banquet for his son. Here the guests just refuse to turn up and even abuse the servants who invited them. The king's reaction isn't just to invite in outsiders ('the bad as well as the good'), but to punish the original invitees. Here is a good example of Jesus the storyteller making use of a powerful parable more than once, adapting it for a different audience and purpose.

Get set

To help with the call and response part of the story, prepare a large placard with the words: 'What's the time, Messy Church?'

Go!

Let me ask a silly question. Who loves a party? Who doesn't love a party?

Call out your favourite party food, party drink, party game, party dance and party goodie-bag present.

Everyone loves a party. So if you get an invitation to a party, it would be very strange to turn it down. You'd have to have a very good reason. And the more important the party, the more you will make every effort to be there... surely?

Once Jesus was invited to a party but, as so often happened with Jesus, he surprised everyone by the things he did and the stories he shared. The people at this party were very exclusive. They'd only invited the best people. And the people who came had to sit in order of importance around the table. Nothing would be allowed to spoil this party. But Jesus took them by surprise.

Jesus wanted them to know about the very best party ever – a much better one than the one they were enjoying. He wanted them to know what God's party was like, what heaven is like, and who would be there.

Jesus decided it was time for a story.

Teach and invite everyone to learn a call and response, namely: 'What's the time, Messy Church?' to which the response initially is, 'It's time for a story!'

Storyteller: What's the time, Messy Church?
Everyone: It's time for a story!

Practise this call and response but switch it around. Use the placard you have prepared to help the congregation know what to say when.

Everyone: What's the time, Messy Church?
Storyteller: It's time for a story!
Storyteller: What's the time, Messy Church?
Everyone: It's time for a story!

Everyone: What's the time, Messy Church?
Storyteller: It's party time!
Storyteller: What's the time, Messy Church?
Everyone: It's party time!

Once there was a rich man who decided to hold a great party – the biggest party ever. He let everyone know and invited everyone to come.

Everyone: What's the time, Messy Church?
Storyteller: It's preparation time!
Storyteller: What's the time, Messy Church?
Everyone: It's preparation time!

The rich man got all his servants working hard. They set the tables with the finest silver cutlery; they put out the very best dinner plates; they polished the most sparkling glassware; and there were lots of really beautiful decorations. And then they set about cooking the best food ever. It was going to be the best party ever. When everything was prepared, he sent out his servant to say that they should come now and enjoy the feast.

Everyone: What's the time, Messy Church?
Storyteller: It's party time!
Storyteller: What's the time, Messy Church?
Everyone: It's party time!

But then the strangest thing happened. The people who had been invited said the strangest things.

Everyone: What's the time, Messy Church?
Storyteller: It's property time!
Storyteller: What's the time, Messy Church?
Everyone: It's property time!

Some decided they had property they needed to go and see; a field they had bought; a new plot of land for a house in the village; an allotment they needed to inspect. They were too busy to come.

Everyone: What's the time, Messy Church?
Storyteller: It's possessions time!
Storyteller: What's the time, Messy Church?
Everyone: It's possessions time!

Some decided they had things they needed to go and look at; a new car they wanted to test-drive; new clothes they wanted to try on; a new iPad they wanted to play with. They were too busy to come.

Everyone: What's the time, Messy Church?
Storyteller: It's partner time!
Storyteller: What's the time, Messy Church?
Everyone: It's partner time!

Some decided they had people to meet; a girlfriend to take out; a client to wine and dine; a friend to meet down the pub. They were too busy to come.

The man who had arranged the best party ever couldn't believe his ears. He was furious (and sad at the same time). They were turning down his invitation.

Everyone: What's the time, Messy Church?
Storyteller: It's party time!
Storyteller: What's the time, Messy Church?
Everyone: It's party time!

So the man who had prepared the best party ever sent his servant out to find new people to invite.

Everyone: What's the time, Messy Church?
Storyteller: It's people-who-are-lonely time!
Everyone: What's the time, Messy Church?
Storyteller: It's people-who-are-poor time!
Everyone: What's the time, Messy Church?
Storyteller: It's people-who-are-messy time!

His servants brought in from the streets people who were lonely; people who were poor; and people whose lives were messy. But still there was room at the biggest party ever.

Everyone: What's the time, Messy Church?
Storyteller: It's plenty of room time!
Storyteller: What's the time, Messy Church?
Everyone: It's plenty of room time!

The man who invited everyone to 'the biggest party ever' wanted his house to be full. This party is for everyone who accepts his invitation. This party is the best party ever. This party is for you and for me, for ever.

Now who would turn down an invitation like that?

Prayer idea

In this prayer, when the leader says the words **too busy**, everyone should groan; when he or she says the word **party**, everyone should cheer.

Practise this.

> Father God, we're sorry that we are often **too busy** to think about you.
>
> But thank you that your love has prepared **a party** for everyone.
>
> Father God, we're sorry that possessions, property and even people often make us **too busy** to think about coming to your **party**.
>
> Father God, thank you for this story of Jesus that reminds us that you are never **too busy** to care about us and that you want us to enjoy life with you, which is the beginning of the best **party** ever.
>
> Amen

9 Messy families

The parable of the prodigal son

Jesus continued: 'There was a man who had two sons. The younger one said to his father, "Father, give me my share of the estate." So he divided his property between them.

'Not long after that, the younger son got together all he had, set off for a distant country and there squandered his wealth in wild living. After he had spent everything, there was a severe famine in that whole country, and he began to be in need. So he went and hired himself out to a citizen of that country, who sent him to his fields to feed pigs. He longed to fill his stomach with the pods that the pigs were eating, but no one gave him anything.

'When he came to his senses, he said, "How many of my father's hired servants have food to spare, and here I am starving to death! I will set out and go back to my father and say to him: Father, I have sinned against heaven and against you. I am no longer worthy to be called your son; make me like one of your hired servants." So he got up and went to his father.

'But while he was still a long way off, his father saw him and was filled with compassion for him; he ran to his son, threw his arms around him and kissed him.

'The son said to him, "Father, I have sinned against heaven and against you. I am no longer worthy to be called your son."

'But the father said to his servants, "Quick! Bring the best robe and put it on him. Put a ring on his finger and sandals on his feet. Bring the fattened calf and kill it. Let's have a feast and celebrate. For this son of mine was dead and is alive again; he was lost and is found." So they began to celebrate.

'Meanwhile, the older son was in the field. When he came near the house, he heard music and dancing. So he called one of the servants and asked him what was going on. "Your brother has come," he replied, "and your father has killed the fattened calf because he has him back safe and sound."

'The older brother became angry and refused to go in. So his father went out and pleaded with him. But he answered his father, "Look! All these years I've been slaving for you and never disobeyed your orders. Yet you never gave me even a young goat so I could celebrate with my friends. But when this son of yours who has squandered your property with prostitutes comes home, you kill the fattened calf for him!"

'"My son," the father said, "you are always with me, and everything I have is yours. But we had to celebrate and be glad, because this brother of yours was dead and is alive again; he was lost and is found."'

LUKE 15:11–32

Get ready

This is part of a block of three lost-and-found parables that Jesus used with both the tax collectors and the religious leaders to explore the all-welcoming love of God. Both groups were 'lost' in different ways. All down history, religious people have tended to become caught up with worrying who is 'in' and who is 'out'. This story challenges all that.

Both the younger and the older son had become distanced from their father in different ways. The father in this parable, like God, loves both and goes out to meet them where they are. Clearly there had been little love between the two sons right from the start. The younger son insults his dad and then escapes from the whole family and the farm, while the older son comes over as a rather pious sort at the end and even refers to his younger brother as 'this son of yours'. This parable comes within a long tradition of stories of sibling rivalry throughout the Bible, but Jesus twists it to say something new and startling to his audience about God.

The younger son offers to become one of his father's hired servants, who were the lowest of the low in a household. His return home and his sorrow may or may not have been whole-hearted but it is worth noticing that the father runs to embrace him even before he can get any words of repentance out. The father's unconditional welcome home is also evidenced by the gifts he gave – a robe, a ring and sandals (servants normally went barefooted) – and the extravagant party he threw. The father had never given up hope that his younger son would come home. He had never disowned nor forgotten about him, but had just waited patiently. And when the son does come back, there are remarkably no words of rebuke or anger; he doesn't say 'I told you so' but offers an extravagant welcome. He is fully accepted back into the family just like all of us with our messy lives, who are welcomed back to God through the ministry of Jesus. This is such a powerful picture for how much God loves each of us.

As so often, Jesus doesn't give any explanation of what this parable means but lets it speak for itself. And most importantly, we don't know how the story ends; does the older son come into the party or not? This is a parable that asks its hearers both then and now to step into the story for themselves and find their place within its drama. The whole point is to ask ourselves what God is saying to us from this story.

Get set

You will need several different sorts of footwear to tell this version of the story: two pairs of mens' wellingtons, one larger and one smaller; some walking boots; some posh city shoes; some mens' dancing shoes; a pair of golden shoes (spray paint an old pair); some grubby sandals; some running shoes; and some new sandals in a shoe box.

Go!

Introduce the different characters and actions in the story by a different pair of shoes each time as indicated in between the text. Line these up, pair by pair, left to right as seen by the congregation. Also, include some crowd sound effects in your story, for example walking, partying, groans, sounds of disgust about the pig food and finally cheers.

Jesus used to welcome anybody and everybody to be his friends; even people others thought didn't deserve his welcome. And this upset some important leaders who thought it was all wrong and that he should really only mix with those who lived good lives, not people whose lives were messy.

To help them understand how big God's love is, Jesus told them this story:

Once there was a farmer who had two sons.

An older son…

Large wellingtons.

And a younger son…

Smaller wellingtons.

Now, the younger son became impatient with living on the farm and wanted to get away. He decided to ask his father for his half of the farm's money, and he wanted it now; he wasn't prepared to wait until his father died. (What impudence!)

The father loved both his sons. Out of love he decided not to get angry with the younger son and force him to stay, but gave him the money that would have come to him one day.

The younger son got himself ready and set off in his walking boots towards the big city.

Walking boots.

When he got there, it was spend, spend, spend! He had plenty of money and soon he had plenty of friends.

He bought himself a pair of posh city shoes.

Smart shoes.

He went out dancing every evening and had a great time.

Shiny dancing shoes.

He was known for luxury and extravagance right down to his golden shoes, in which he would walk around town.

Golden shoes.

It seemed as if the good times would go on forever, but then disaster struck. A famine hit the land.

The crops failed; prices rose; and the economy went into deep depression.

What was worse: the son's money ran out. And his friends left him.

He walked away from the city in a pair of grubby shoes, to find work where he could.

Grubby shoes.

The only job he could find was feeding pigs for a farmer. It was smelly and dirty in the pigsty. And sometimes he was so hungry, he even thought of eating the pig food.

He couldn't even afford any shoes now.

This young man had sunk really low. And it was only then that he slowly came to his senses. He remembered how good things had been on his father's farm. Even the servants there had a better life than his life now.

He decided to go home, to say sorry and to ask his dad to take him on as a hired servant.

He's now barefooted. Invite someone to take off his/her shoes and socks, and walk slowly like the son returning home.

Guess what? All this time, the father had been looking out for his son. He had never given up hope that he would return one day.

And when the son was still some way off, his dad saw him and put on his running shoes…

Running shoes.

… hitched up his long cloak, and ran to meet his son. And before the son could say much, he wrapped his arms around him and gave him the biggest hug of welcome ever.

He was so happy to have his son home – the son he thought he had lost; the son who could so easily have been dead but was alive and found.

He put new clothes on him; gave him a special ring to show he was truly back in the family again; and gave him a new expensive pair of sandals to wear.

New sandals out of a shoebox.

And he threw the biggest welcome home party ever.

Three cheers for the son who was lost and who is found!

Three cheers.

Meanwhile, the older son, who was working out in the fields, heard all this noise.

Move the large wellingtons from the start of the story to the end.

He found out what was happening and was angry. He was angry that his father was showing such love to his brother who had thrown away so much of the farm's money.

The father went out to him… and said this: 'Son, I've always loved you too. You've never lacked anything. All that I have is yours. But it's right we celebrate your brother's return. He was lost and now is found; he was dead and now he's alive.'

And the older brother said…

I wonder what he said, because that's when Jesus ended the story.

Point to the larger wellingtons.

I wonder what you would have done in the older brother's shoes?

Would you have welcomed your runaway brother?

Would you have forgiven him?

Would you have wanted the father to hold you just like he hugged the returning son?

And I wonder who is like God in this story?

And I wonder who is like you… and what this story says to you today?

Prayer idea

Use hand actions (far, long, wide and big) to explore God's love in a prayer.

Practise:

How far *(point both hands forward into the distance)* the younger son had gone away.

How long *(reach up with one hand and down with the other)* the father had waited.

How wide *(stretch the arms wide)* was God's love.

How big *(hold a huge, heavy 'present' of grace in your hands)* is God's welcome and love and grace for each one of us.

Let's pray:

> We are sorry that we have so often run **far** away from you and gone **far** from your love.
> Thank you that you have waited a **long** time for us.
> Thank you that your love is so **wide.**
> Thank you that your gifts to us are so many and so **big**.
> Amen

10 Messy fishing

The parable of the fish caught in the net

[Jesus continued,] 'Once again, the kingdom of heaven is like a net that was let down into the lake and caught all kinds of fish. When it was full, the fishermen pulled it up on the shore. Then they sat down and collected the good fish in baskets, but threw the bad away. This is how it will be at the end of the age. The angels will come and separate the wicked from the righteous and throw them into the blazing furnace, where there will be weeping and gnashing of teeth.

'Have you understood all these things?' Jesus asked.

MATTHEW 13:47–51

Get ready

This short story is sometimes overlooked. However, of all the parables, it is probably one that made most immediate sense to Jesus' fishermen followers. The sifting of a catch of fish would have been a common sight on the shores of Galilee. Galilee contained many types of fish as well as other sorts of sea creatures that might have been caught in a drag net. One of the fish still caught today (the Musht) is known locally as St Peter's fish, linked to the story of Peter finding a coin for his taxes in a fish he caught on Jesus' instructions (Matthew 17:27).

A drag net was long and hung from floats just beneath the water's surface. It was held in place by two boats that slowly hauled it to shore. This helps to explain why Andrew and Peter needed to work with James and John in partnership to get a good catch.

Jesus is comparing the mixed catch of fish to the way all sorts were being welcomed into the kingdom of God. It was a real intergenerational, multicultural and interfaith collection of people from all walks of life. Any sorting out of this mix, though, only comes later and is not the church's responsibility. The last judgement is outside its remit and in the hands of heaven (the angels). Christians all too readily set themselves up as the judges of who are 'insiders' and who are 'outsiders'. This is not their job.

The parable ends with a frightening image of judgement that many today find disturbing. However, we need to remember that Jesus, like many a great storyteller (think of Grimm's fairy tales), is using deliberately shocking language to capture his audience's attention. What matters is, what sort of fish will we be? This is what Jesus urgently wants us to consider.

Get set

No particular props are needed for this parable retelling, unless you just happen to have some fun model fish easily to hand.

Go!

Are you ready for a fishy tale?

Maybe we should get into the mood by becoming fish swimming in a Messy Church aquarium.

Encourage some fish actions on the spot from everyone. Whenever particular fish are mentioned in the story, set this off again.

It's not much fun being a fish.

Round and round we swim.

Up and down we swim.

In and out we swim.

And all to end up exactly where we started! Though getting back there, it seems like somewhere new.

Our fish memories are not too hot, you know.

And maybe this is a good thing. If the last time you found that rock… that piece of weed… was more than seconds ago, then we will have forgotten all about it and it will be like discovering something new for the first time!

What a life we fish live!

I know there's Nemo and Dory, but they're not real fish. They've got names for a start… and memories (of a sort).

There are just lots of different types of us fish, and there are millions of types.

Even on the Sea of Galilee where Jesus told stories, there are lots of varieties of fish. All sorts swam beneath the surface of the lake.

Take the sardines, for example. Two little ones ended up in a boy's picnic once and made history by producing the biggest fish snack ever. Not bad for two tiddlers!

And there's the Musht fish, known in many countries as the tilapia. One of these hit the headlines once too, when Peter caught one on his fishing rod and, guess what, there was a coin in its mouth, just enough to pay Peter's taxes. A financial fish. The fish with the golden gill.

This fish goes by the name of St Peter's fish today. It's great for tourism.

And there are more, so many more: damsel fish, mouthbreeder fish, biny fish, barbel fish and catfish.

The fishermen of Jesus' day knew all about fish. It was their job, after all.

Well, it used to be, until Jesus called them to be 'fishers of men'. Then the 'fish' did get names, like Zacchaeus and Jairus, like Martha, Mary and Lazarus, like… you and me.

Catching fish for everyday life and catching people for eternal life were their life-long jobs.

Once Jesus said God's kingdom was like a great fishing net welcoming all on board – the Damsel fish, the Mouthbreeder fish, the Biny fish, the Barbel fish, the Musht fish, the Catfish and the Sardines. All swimming into God's loving arms.

Only God knows which fish are ready to be caught.

Only God knows which fish are good on the inside.

Only God knows which fish will end up in heaven.

In the meantime, we're all in the business of fishing with God.

Fishing for all sorts: big and small; young and old; beautiful and not so beautiful; fish of this colour or that colour; fish of this type or that.

God loves to welcome all sorts of fishy people into his kingdom.

All God asks is, are you ready to swim into his net of love?

So, I wonder, on a fishy scale of one to ten, are you ready… are you willing to be caught up with God?

Prayer idea

The first Christians used the sign of the fish as a secret way of identifying who was a follower of Jesus during times of persecution. They used an elongated Greek letter Alpha, which looks like a fish, and the Greek letters for the word fish stood for 'Jesus Christ Son of God Saviour'.

Teach this letter shape, which people can draw in the air, as their 'amen' to the following 'fish prayer' if they wish.

F – Father, *f*orgive us for the way our lives have not been the best you planned them to be.
Amen

I – Thank you for *i*nviting us to be part of your kingdom.
Amen

S – Thank you for sending Jesus to be our *s*aviour and friend.
Amen

H – *H*elp us to serve and follow you in the week ahead.
Amen

11
Messy forgiveness

The parable of the unforgiving servant

Then Peter came to Jesus and asked, 'Lord, how many times shall I forgive my brother or sister who sins against me? Up to seven times?'

Jesus answered, 'I tell you, not seven times, but seventy-seven times.

'Therefore, the kingdom of heaven is like a king who wanted to settle accounts with his servants. As he began the settlement, a man who owed him ten thousand bags of gold was brought to him. Since he was not able to pay, the master ordered that he and his wife and his children and all that he had be sold to repay the debt.

'At this the servant fell on his knees before him. "Be patient with me," he begged, "and I will pay back everything." The servant's master took pity on him, cancelled the debt and let him go.

'But when that servant went out, he found one of his fellow servants who owed him a hundred silver coins. He grabbed him and began to choke him. "Pay back what you owe me!" he demanded.

'His fellow servant fell to his knees and begged him, "Be patient with me, and I will pay it back."

'But he refused. Instead, he went off and had the man thrown into prison until he could pay the debt. When the other servants saw what had happened, they were outraged and went and told their master everything that had happened.

'Then the master called the servant in. "You wicked servant," he said, "I cancelled all that debt of yours because you begged me to. Shouldn't you have had mercy on your fellow servant just as I had on you?" In anger his master handed him over to the jailers to be tortured, until he should pay back all he owed.

'This is how my heavenly Father will treat each of you unless you forgive your brother or sister from your heart.'

MATTHEW 18:21–35

Get ready

The suggestion that we should forgive others, as is contained within the Lord's Prayer, is surely an impossible idea. What about the real world where people hurt others again and again? Some actions are unforgiveable, aren't they? This is at the heart of the very practical question that Peter puts to Jesus before this story. It is a story about what it is like in God's scheme of things – God's kingdom – to which we are called. The truth is we are all like the servant who owed millions. There are so many reasons why we are in no position to be 'friends of the king', but God's mercy makes forgiveness possible. The servant is forgiven, but then this forgiveness should be passed on. Peter and the others who heard the story for the first time would have reacted with anger at the way the pardoned servant treated those who owed him money. It's obvious that those who receive mercy should pass it on and so Peter has his answer.

The amounts of money used in this story are ridiculous and would have made the crowds laugh. The servant owed the equivalent of 50,000 lifetimes-worth of wages, whereas the amount the man owed him was only three months' wages. However, this isn't just exaggeration for comic effect. It underlines how huge our debt to God is compared with our mutual hurts and grievances. Because of God's love generously poured out to us in Jesus, we are forgiven and, as we are reminded in the Lord's Prayer, this means we should forgive others.

Lack of forgiveness can tear apart communities, churches and families. It has been suggested that the brother that Peter is talking about might be his own blood brother Andrew; to offer and receive forgiveness within your own family is often the hardest place of all. The king's servant in the story actually says, in the Greek, 'Pay your debts!' to his own servant. Like many of us, he may have been morally in the right... but so heartless.

This extended and memorable parable builds on Jesus' own short commentary on the Lord's Prayer in Matthew 6:14. The line about forgiveness in that prayer is the one part Jesus clearly felt needed a special underlining.

Get set

You will need: a blow-up die with the following half sentences printed off as labels and attached over the numbers:

1 I find it hard to forgive others when...
2 I find it hard to forgive others because...
3 I find... unforgivable.
4 I would forgive others but...
5 I can only forgive others if...
6 My limit for forgiving others would be... times

Also have some coins and paper strips to make prayer chains.

Go!

Introduce the topic of forgiveness by showing the die you have created (see above), throwing it and inviting your congregation to complete the sentence on the face that falls uppermost. This should get some discussion going.

Jesus once told a story about forgiveness.

It was because his friend Peter had asked how many times we can reasonably go on forgiving people. Is there a limit? Seven times? 70 times?

To everyone's shock, Jesus said there should be no limit. He told a story to explain why.

To make the point of this parable very visible, pile up lots of coins of different denominations on one side of a table – include some notes if you dare – and another, but much smaller, pile of just a few pence on the other side. Point to the two piles as you retell the story.

A lot of money… a little bit of money.

A lot of debt… a tiny debt.

Owing a massive amount… owing just a few pence.

So Jesus told a story. There was once a king who called his chief servants together.

It was time to audit their accounts, to see how well they had looked after the king's money.

One servant had stepped way out of line.

He owed billions and billions of pounds. He was in deep trouble. He could never repay. He was facing a life in prison and confiscation of all his family property.

But guess what?

He said sorry. He asked the king for time to pay. He threw himself on the king's mercy.

And, amazingly, the king forgave him for his massive debt.

You don't mean it? Yes, the king forgave him. He let him off the lot.

How grateful that man must have felt, how relieved. He had got his life back.

So what did he do?

Well, when he bumped into one of his own servants who owed him just a few pence, he…

… forgave him?

… showed him mercy?

… let him off his debt?

NO! He was furious. He had that man put in prison until he had paid it all back in full.

Can you believe it? What sort of gratitude was that?

And when the king heard, he was mad. 'I forgave you billions and you wouldn't even let your servant off a few pence?

'What were you thinking, man?

'Couldn't you show some mercy like I did?

'Couldn't you let him off just as I let you off?

'That's it. I've had enough of you. To prison with you until every penny is paid. It will take for ever!'

Jesus turned to the crowds.

Such a huge debt… such a small debt.

So much to forgive… so little to forgive.

Do you get it?

Do you get how important it is to forgive?

Do you see how much God has forgiven you?

So go and do the same. However many times you need to say 'I forgive you', it's never enough to match how much God has forgiven you.

Prayer idea

Friendship is forgiving... but forgiving others doesn't come easily. It's like building a paper chain, link by link. Every time we forgive, we strengthen the possibility of an eventual total link-up.

In a time of prayer, create some forgiveness paper chains. Invite everyone to write on the chains some symbols or words for those things that build barriers between people, such as: distrust, harsh words, fear, ignorance, unfairness, jealousy, hurt and anger.

Now connect up the links to make a long paper chain.

When you have linked up all the links of the chain, invite everyone to draw a very deliberate cross over each word, picture or sentence to remember how Jesus has forgiven us for all these things and how this is the source of our strength to link up in friendship and forgiveness with others.

Hold the chain as a group and pray together the key line from the Lord's Prayer:

Forgive us for doing wrong as we forgive others.
MATTHEW 6:12, CEV

12
Messy friends

The parable of the friend at midnight

Then Jesus said to them: 'Suppose you have a friend. You go to him at midnight and say, "Friend, lend me three loaves of bread. A friend of mine on a journey has come to stay with me. I have no food to give him." And suppose the one inside answers, "Don't bother me. The door is already locked. My children and I are in bed. I can't get up and give you anything." I tell you, that person will not get up. And he won't give you bread just because he is your friend. But because you keep bothering him, he will surely get up. He will give you as much as you need.

'So here is what I say to you. Ask, and it will be given to you. Search, and you will find. Knock, and the door will be opened to you. Everyone who asks will receive. The one who searches will find. And the door will be opened to the one who knocks.'
LUKE 11:5–10 (NIRV)

Get ready

This story comes as part of a longer piece that acts as a commentary on Luke's version of the Lord's Prayer (vv. 2–4) and that, in turn, is prompted by the fact that one unnamed disciple had asked Jesus how to pray. In Luke's overall story it also connects with the story of Mary and Martha in the previous chapter. Prayer is, at heart, resting at the feet of our heavenly Father, listening more than talking.

Jesus unpacks his model prayer further with two stories about the respective responses of first a friend and then a parent to requests for help. How much more readily will God answer our prayers than a reluctant friend at midnight or an earthly father? The emphasis is on God's readiness to hear our prayers but this is balanced out with our responsibility to be persistent – to ask, seek and knock.

The Lord's Prayer, as it is recorded in Luke's Gospel, is short, simple and direct. It reminds us that we don't need complicated words, fine sentences or complex theology to pray. This is good news for Messy Churches and all of us. The other good news is that Jesus says 'everyone who asks will receive'. What we receive will be what is best for us, not always what we think we need. This comes out clearly a few verses further on when Jesus promises that God will give us his Holy Spirit (v. 13) – more of God is always what we all need.

Get set

You will need something wooden on which to knock and in particular a surface that gives a good loud echo.

Go!

Begin your retelling with a few traditional 'knock knock' jokes. You can find plenty online and your congregation will probably come up with a few as well, if invited.

Knock… knock… knock… knock…

Knocking on a door is the main sound effect in today's parable. Let's all do some door knocking.

Invite everyone to join in and to do so every time you mention 'knocking'.

So much knocking!

Most people respond quite quickly to a knock on the door and open the door to a visitor, if they are at home. But Jesus told a story about a man knocking on the door of his friend's house at midnight. What sort of hour is that for visiting?

I wonder how long he had to knock for?

I wonder how long the man inside pretended not to hear?

I wonder how many times he said in his head, 'Go away'?

But his friend didn't go away and eventually the homeowner did shout, 'Go away. We're all in bed. It's late. Stop knocking.'

His friend didn't stop. Instead he called out, 'Someone's arrived late and needs food. I've nothing in the house. Can I have some bread?'

Is that really a reason to knock someone awake at midnight? What do you think?

But the friend was so persistent. It was like some terrible torture.

Knock… knock… knock… knock…

The man did not give up. In what sort of mood was the man inside the house by now, do you think? Friend or no friend…?

Finally… eventually… he got up and opened the door.

I wonder if there was a smile on his face? Would you have smiled? There are perhaps limits to friendship; even friendship can be pushed too far.

He did give him some bread, though.

But don't you see? God is your best friend ever; God would get up straight away. God wouldn't hesitate to open the door to you to give you what you need.

So just keep on asking and God will give you what you need.

So just keep on looking for his response and God will show you what's next.

So just keep on knocking and God will be there for you.

Prayer is about knocking on God's door and we never have to wait long. Why?

Well, the truth is that God's been knocking on our door for ages already. Prayer is a two-way process.

God has gifts to give to you. And the very best gift God has to give – the gift we all need – is God himself, the gift of his Holy Spirit in our hearts.

So go on asking; go on looking; go on knocking for this gift.

This is prayer.

Prayer idea

Why not introduce the Lord's Prayer to your Messy Church congregation? Teach the words of this prayer of knocking on God's door and then say them together.

It may help everyone to teach some simple actions to accompany each line. There are some signing suggestions on the Messy Church Pinterest page: **www.pinterest.com/MessyChurchBRF**

13
Messy gifts

The parable of the talents

[Jesus said: 'The kingdom of God] will be like a man going on a journey, who called his servants and entrusted his wealth to them. To one he gave five bags of gold, to another two bags, and to another one bag, each according to his ability. Then he went on his journey. The man who had received five bags of gold went at once and put his money to work and gained five bags more. So also, the one with two bags of gold gained two more. But the man who had received one bag went off, dug a hole in the ground and hid his master's money.

'After a long time the master of those servants returned and settled accounts with them. The man who had received five bags of gold brought the other five. "Master," he said, "you entrusted me with five bags of gold. See, I have gained five more."

'His master replied, "Well done, good and faithful servant! You have been faithful with a few things; I will put you in charge of many things. Come and share your master's happiness!"

'The man with two bags of gold also came. "Master," he said, "you entrusted me with two bags of gold; see, I have gained two more."

'His master replied, "Well done, good and faithful servant! You have been faithful with a few things; I will put you in charge of many things. Come and share your master's happiness!"

'Then the man who had received one bag of gold came. "Master," he said, "I knew that you are a hard man, harvesting where you have not sown and gathering where you have not scattered seed. So I was afraid and went out and hid your gold in the ground. See, here is what belongs to you."

'His master replied, "You wicked, lazy servant! So you knew that I harvest where I have not sown and gather where I have not scattered seed? Well then, you should have put my money on deposit with the bankers, so that when I returned I would have received it back with interest.

'"So take the bag of gold from him and give it to the one who has ten bags. For whoever has will be given more, and they will have an abundance. Whoever does not have, even what they have will be taken from them. And throw that worthless servant outside, into the darkness, where there will be weeping and gnashing of teeth."'

MATTHEW 25:14–30

Get ready

This parable comes near the end of Jesus' earthly ministry during Holy Week and its focus explores the question of what it means to be a faithful servant of God. There is a similar but distinctive version of this parable in Luke's Gospel (Luke 19:11–27). The basic storyline is the same in both and perhaps this suggests that Jesus used the same story on more than one occasion but with variations. Each also revolves around the return of a prince or a master at the end of the story. It may be that both parables were of particular significance to the first Christians as it helped throw some light on their questions about Jesus' promised second coming.

The story tackles a key question, namely: 'What are we to do with God's gift of life to us?' or 'How should we live this life best while waiting for Jesus to return?' As parables, however, they do contain some difficulties for us. Money is used to represent each person's gift and it's hard for some to see beyond this to what it might really mean. The translation 'bags of gold' in the passage above represents the word 'talent'. A talent was a large amount of money equivalent to 20 years' wages. In each story it is financial profit that is offered as a picture of faithfulness with life's gift, and this can also present a stumbling block to understanding the parable.

In Matthew's story there are three servants, who were given varying amounts of money, whereas in Luke's version there are ten, although the focus is on only three at the end. In Luke's story the context, within which each does his best with the amounts given, is one of hostility to themselves and the kingdom. The element of judgement in both is also intriguing. In Matthew, the judgement falls on one of those servants, whereas in Luke it also falls on the nobleman's enemies. The rewards are also different. In Matthew, the reward is money, whereas in Luke's story it is a reward of responsibility over cities.

Finally, as so often with the parables, we are left with a genuine but puzzling thought about why it should not have been regarded as a faithful thing to have kept something safe and simply given back the 'trust' intact to the master on his return. The one who does this earns condemnation rather than a 'well done'. There is a lot to wonder about in this parable and maybe even the first Christians also struggled to understand what it meant.

Get set

The following version of the story involves people moving whenever certain key words are mentioned.

The key words are: *servant; gold; master; well done; more; put in charge; happiness.*

Write these words/phrases large on placards and then assign different sections of your Messy congregation to each.

Practise calling out the words randomly, upon which each group should stand and then sit down again. You could also negotiate a particular action to go with each word/phrase, such as: miming putting on a grand robe for 'master', or handing a document of authority over for 'put in charge'. At the very least, each group could cheer when they stand.

Keep the story moving at a good pace, pausing before the key words/ phrases sometimes as if to try and catch the groups out. Make it fun!

Go!

Once, Jesus told a story to help people work out what the kingdom of God is like:

Once upon a time a *master* had three *servants*. The *master* was going off on a long journey, so he called his three *servants* to see him. He gave the first five bags of *gold* to look after; he gave the second two bags of *gold*; and he gave the third *servant* just one bag to look after.

As soon as the *master* was gone the first one took his five bags of *gold* and used it to make *more* money. Very soon this *servant* had made five *more* bags of *gold*.

The second man with his two bags also worked hard with the money and made two *more* bags of yellow coins.

But the third *servant* took his one bag of *gold* and hid it away. He didn't make any *more* money. He thought it would be best to keep his *master*'s *gold* safe for his return.

When the *master* returned he called the three together. The first one said, 'Look, here are your five bags and here are five *more*.' '*Well done*,' said the *master*. 'I will *put you in charge* of *more* and you can come and share in my *happiness*.'

The second man said, 'Look, here are your two bags of **gold** and here are two **more**.' '**Well done**,' said the boss. 'I will **put you in charge** of **more** and you can come and share in my **happiness**.'

Finally the third **servant** came. He said, 'I knew you were a hard **master** and that you wouldn't want any **gold** lost, so I hid my bag in the ground. Here is your one bag of **gold**. No less and no **more**!'

The **master** was furious. He said, 'My first **servant** made five **more** bags; my second **servant** made an extra two bags of **gold**. For that reason they are **in charge** of **more**. But you have only one bag still. You didn't make any **more**. You could have at least put the **gold** in the bank and made some interest!

'No **well done** for you. You don't deserve to be **put in charge** and you won't share my **happiness**. Give the one bag of **gold** to the **servant** with five bags. Everyone who makes **more** will gain **more**, but anyone who doesn't make **more** with what they have will lose what they have and not share my **happiness**!'

Phew, that was exhausting… but also fun!

But what was it all about, do you think?

Was Jesus saying to his followers that we need to be good with money?

Or is it not about money?

And what about if…

… the last man had said: 'I went into business with my bag but the business failed and I lost the lot'… or, 'I was on my way to the city to invest it, but it was all stolen'… or, 'I was on my way to the market and I saw a beggar in great need, so I gave the bag away'.

What do you think the master would have said then?

Invite some comment and ideas.

I wonder what truly earns God's **well done**… will **put us in charge**… of **more**… and bring us into God's **happiness**? I wonder what is worth more than **gold** to God… if we choose to be God's **servant** and make God our true **master**?

Prayer idea

We use the word 'talent' (which meant money in the time of Jesus) to mean a special gift today. That is all because of this parable. Our talents are gifts from God, just as in the story.

Ask everyone to get into small groups and, after a short time to think, to let each other know what they think the other's talents/special gifts are. Other people usually recognise these better than we can ourselves.

Now make this a big prayer of thanks to God, as you finish the following short prayer below with everyone calling out the talent that the others have identified as theirs:

Thank you, Father God, for making each of us special and giving us the talent of…
    Help us not to hide it but to use it to bless others and bring joy to you.
Amen

14
Messy harvest

The parable of the wheat and the weeds

Jesus told them another parable: 'The kingdom of heaven is like a man who sowed good seed in his field. But while everyone was sleeping, his enemy came and sowed weeds among the wheat, and went away. When the wheat sprouted and formed heads, then the weeds also appeared.

'The owner's servants came to him and said, "Sir, didn't you sow good seed in your field? Where then did the weeds come from?"

'"An enemy did this," he replied.

'The servants asked him, "Do you want us to go and pull them up?"

'"No," he answered, "because while you are pulling up the weeds, you may uproot the wheat with them. Let both grow together until the harvest. At that time I will tell the harvesters: First collect the weeds and tie them in bundles to be burned; then gather the wheat and bring it into my barn."'

MATTHEW 13:24–30

Get ready

The Bible has lots of harvest stories. In the Middle East there were two harvests – an early and a late one – so harvest was very much part of their lives. And because life then depended so much on what the ground could produce (and not on what is on special offer at the supermarket), the harvest was always a very special time indeed. Harvest reminded the people then, and also can remind us today, of something amazing in God's creation – that most of the things that we eat have come from the tiniest of seeds. It's no wonder that Jesus used seeds in so many of his parables – each one designed to get us thinking more about what God is like and who we are meant to be. These parables can be puzzling, however, and the parable of the weeds and wheat was certainly meant to challenge his listeners then and now.

This is one of the two parables of Jesus where we have an explanation of its meaning, the other being the parable of the sower. It used to be said that parables (the Greek word literally means 'a comparison') were stories that had only one key teaching point. However, Jesus' own explanation for these two parables unpacks them more as allegories where there are depths of meaning. In the explanation given in verses 36 to 43, every part of the parable stands for someone or something. This is an exemplar from Jesus for his disciples of how to listen to his parables properly and understand them, allowing them perhaps to teach both the disciples and us many things about the kingdom of God.

This parable also addresses two other big questions for his disciples then and now: namely, why is there evil (bad seed) in this world; and should they be the ones to sort out the bad from the good – in other words, become judges of who's in and who's out in God's kingdom? Clearly an enemy, identified as the devil, has been at work in God's creation but the final sort-out – the harvest – is in God's hands not theirs, nor ours. One day all evil will be defeated and destroyed and 'the good seed people' will be safe. The description given by Jesus of the latter in his explanation (Matthew 13:43) recalls Daniel's prophecy in Daniel 12:3: 'Those who are wise will shine like the brightness of the heavens, and those who lead many to righteousness, like the stars for ever and ever.'

The weed referred to in this parable is a poisonous plant called darnel, which looks very similar to wheat until it is fully grown – hence the reluctance to pull it up before the harvest. Compared to other religious teachers and movements of his day, Jesus wasn't quick to decide who was a true follower and who wasn't – he simply welcomed all. There would be a time for judgement when the end came, but not before. And anyway, unlike the darnel, people can change.

Get set

For this story you will need to print off the set of photos from slides available to download at **www.messychurch.org.uk/5504**.

Alternatively, you could collect and use similar pictures of your own from the internet, calendars or books.

Beware rushing into giving your interpretation of this parable as you share it, or even saying what Jesus says about it later in Matthew 13. Give the Messy congregation time to talk about it in groups together first.

Encourage everyone to listen to what the Holy Spirit is saying through this story for now.

Go!

Today's parable is a harvest story.

To help us get into the swing of it, let's try becoming a human harvesting machine.

Invite people to get into mixed-age groups of four.

Each of you is going to become part of the harvest process with appropriate sound effects.

1 Sowing
2 Watering
3 Inspecting
4 Cutting

The sower should be scattering the seeds and humming away happily; the waterer should become a mechanical hose with outstretched arms as the water is fountained out over the fields, plus water noises; the inspectors should be lifting the ears of corn pronouncing their verdict, for example, 'This one is ripening well; this one's a poor specimen' and so on; and finally, the cutters should become great combine harvesters – noisy and with blades (hands) cutting away powerfully.

Practise each part separately and then set in motion a host of human harvesting machines.

Jesus told this story:

Show picture 1 of furrows: The kingdom of heaven is like what happens when a farmer scatters good seed in a field.

Show picture 2 of green shoots: But while everyone was sleeping, an enemy came and scattered weed seeds in the field and then left.

Show picture 3 of a field of corn: When the plants came up and began to ripen, the farmer's servants could see the weeds.

Show picture 4 of weeds and wheat: The servants came and asked: 'Sir, didn't you scatter good seed in your field? Where did these weeds come from?'

'An enemy did this,' he replied.

His servants then asked: 'Do you want us to go out and pull up the weeds?'

'No!' he answered. 'You might also pull up the wheat. Leave the weeds alone until harvest time...'

Show picture 5 of harvest time: '… then I'll tell my workers to gather the weeds and tie them up and burn them…'

Show picture 6 of burned-up stubble: '… but I'll have them store the wheat in my barn.'

Show picture 7 of wondering questions:

I wonder what you like about the story?

I wonder what puzzles you about the story?

I wonder what's the most important part of the story?

I wonder what this story teaches you about God?

I wonder what this story means for you today?

Show picture 8 of flowers in a field while everyone talks about the parable.

Listen to what people have said.

Do you know, people didn't really understand this parable when Jesus first told it? Even his disciples didn't get it. They had to ask him privately what it meant.

But you get it, don't you?

Prayer idea

Show picture 9 with the Bible verse.

Read this together:

> God gives seed to farmers and provides everyone with food. He will increase what you have, so that you can give even more to those in need. You will be blessed in every way, and you will be able to keep on being generous.
> 2 CORINTHIANS 9:10–11 (CEV)

We can turn this into a prayer about wanting to become the good seed in the parable.

Thank you, Lord God, for giving us good seed that we can sow through our words and actions every day.

May what we do and say bless others so there will be a rich harvest of generosity in our homes, our schools, our workplaces and our neighbourhoods.

Through Jesus who is the Lord of the harvest.
Amen

15
Messy justice

The parable of the widow and the judge

Then Jesus told his disciples a parable to show them that they should always pray and not give up. He said: 'In a certain town there was a judge who neither feared God nor cared what people thought. And there was a widow in that town who kept coming to him with the plea, "Grant me justice against my adversary."

'For some time he refused. But finally he said to himself, "Even though I don't fear God or care what people think, yet because this widow keeps bothering me, I will see that she gets justice, so that she won't eventually come and attack me!"'

And the Lord said, 'Listen to what the unjust judge says. And will not God bring about justice for his chosen ones, who cry out to him day and night? Will he keep putting them off? I tell you, he will see that they get justice, and quickly. However, when the Son of Man comes, will he find faith on the earth?'

LUKE 18:1–8

Get ready

This is one of two parables that Luke puts side by side as they both relate to prayer, the other being the story of the Pharisee and the tax collector in the temple. This first story has a lot in common with the parable of the friend at midnight; both serve as a contrast to the speed and willingness with which God answers prayer.

Jesus introduces us to two rather comical, exaggerated and therefore memorable characters for his story. We meet a rogue, godless judge and a nagging widow who just won't give up. The crowds would have recognised these sorts from everyday life in Palestine. Every town had its law court with volunteer judges, some better than others; and every town also had its fair share of widows who had little status or money, since in those days they inherited nothing from their deceased husbands, except perhaps debts. They were easy to spot in their widow's weeds and, although many would have disappeared into the shadows, the widow in this story by contrast was determined not to be pushed aside.

Luke introduces the parable as being about staying persistent in prayer, though in fact it is much more about how ready God is to hear the prayers of 'his chosen ones who cry to him day and night'. It is teaching us more about the God to whom we pray than how to pray.

This is surely an attractive parable for any storyteller who wants to throw himself or herself into voicing the nagging widow and the irritated judge. Jesus must have made his audience both laugh and think with this story, and that makes the sting in the tail even more powerful when Jesus asks: 'Will the Son of Man find faith on earth when he returns?'

Get set

You will need a judge's wig or something similar; a widow's veil, which could be a black shawl you drape over your head and shoulders; and a gavel or something similar.

You could deliver this retelling of the parable as a monologue, changing costume for the different characters each time, or perhaps ask someone to work with you. The story needs to be over the top and played for laughs.

Go!

Bang the makeshift gavel on a table several times.

All rise for His Lordship, the honourable Justice Judge Careless.

Enter Judge Careless.

This court is now in session.

Enter the plaintiff Widow Cranky.

'Oh no,' muttered Judge Careless to himself. 'Not her again; she's been here every day for the past three weeks!'

(With a long sigh) 'Please state your case, Widow Cranky (though we all know it… off by heart!).'

'I'm here for justice, my Lord. You know that what has happened is just not fair. Just because I'm a widow, they've taken advantage of my status. I'm powerless to act. All I want is a fair hearing, my Lord.'

'Hearing! Hearing!' exploded Judge Careless. 'I am always hearing you. Day in, day out! You've been here demanding a hearing for weeks. Look, you've been heard, now go! Case dismissed.'

'But I need you to hear my case, my Lord. I need you to decide in my favour. I need you to put right what is wrong.'

'Right? Wrong? You're the one that needs putting right because you're in the wrong… and that's an end to it! You're driving me mad each day with your whining and moaning, your demanding and pleading. Go away! Just go away.'

'But, my Lord, you're the only one who can help. You're the only one who can hear my case, who can decide my cause.'

'I'm telling you, the only cause I have from you is cause for a headache! Why should I bother with you? I'm Judge Careless, Care-less. Don't you hear? The clue is in the name. I couldn't care less about you. So push off, lady. Case dismissed.'

'That's not fair, my Lord. I am not going. And even if you make me go, I'll be back tomorrow, and the next day and the next. God knows I'm in the right.'

'OK, OK, I get it. You've pushed me to the limit. So, even though I don't care about you, and I don't care about your God… just to get rid of you… I'm finding in your favour. There, you can have your justice. Now go!'

'Thank you, my Lord. But since I'm here, can I just ask you one small favour…?'

'No, no, no! Go away! Court adjourned. Court suspended. Court dismissed. Quick, I'm out of here!'

Now that's the story Jesus told once and everyone laughed and laughed. They loved the two larger-than-life characters involved.

But don't you see what it means, said Jesus?

Even Judge Careless gave in to Widow Cranky's cry for justice…. eventually.

God, on the other hand, always hears our cry. God doesn't need persuading to listen for weeks and weeks on end like this. God always hears our prayer first time and gives us the best answer he can.

So are you praying? Are you talking with God every day?

I seriously wonder, said Jesus, whether there will still be people praying with faith on earth when the end of the world comes.

Is he right, do you think?

Prayer idea

Prayers can take different forms: 'thank you' prayers, 'please help' prayers, 'I'm sorry' prayers, or simple 'here I am listening' prayers.

As this story is about someone who was powerless asking for justice, focus on some 'please help' prayers this time for people locally and globally who are facing hard times.

Invite the congregation to suggest names or particular situations.

As these are called out, say a short 'please help' prayer and then invite everyone to respond:

Lord Jesus, hear our prayer.

16
Messy livestock

The parable of the lost sheep

Then Jesus told them this parable: 'Suppose one of you has a hundred sheep and loses one of them. Doesn't he leave the ninety-nine in the open country and go after the lost sheep until he finds it? And when he finds it, he joyfully puts it on his shoulders and goes home. Then he calls his friends and neighbours together and says, "Rejoice with me; I have found my lost sheep." I tell you that in the same way there will be more rejoicing in heaven over one sinner who repents than over ninety-nine righteous persons who do not need to repent.'
LUKE 15:3–7

[Jesus said,] 'See that you do not despise one of these little ones. For I tell you that their angels in heaven always see the face of my Father in heaven.

'What do you think? If a man owns a hundred sheep, and one of them wanders away, will he not leave the ninety-nine on the hills and go to look for the one that wandered off? And if he finds it, truly I tell you, he is happier about that one sheep than about the ninety-nine that did not wander off. In the same way your Father in heaven is not willing that any of these little ones should perish.'
MATTHEW 18:10–14

The parable of the lost sheep appears twice in the Gospels. In each case, it is set in the context of the way in which Jesus welcomes those people who others don't see as important, be they disreputable tax collectors and sinners as in Luke's version, or 'the little ones', which includes children, as in Matthew's Gospel.

This is such a well-known and much-loved story that it can easily be reduced to a cute tale of the finding of a poor lost sheep. But it isn't just about sheep or even a shepherd, but about God, of course. Jesus is likening himself to God, the good shepherd, and is letting us know the surprising lengths God is willing to go to make sure we are back home safely in the family fold.

Once again there is that dimension of scandal and surprise in the story that we find in so many of the parables of Jesus. The question Jesus poses at the beginning of the parable would have been greeted with howls of derision from his audience. Of course no sensible shepherd would bother. The rich shepherd of the parable should have sent one of his servants to do this messy job but, instead, he himself goes off in search of the one missing sheep. That's crazy. But the ways of God's kingdom are different and God's passionate love for us is 'out of this world'. Everyone matters, whether it is one in 100 or one in the seven billion on our planet.

This story really shows us what sort of God Jesus was talking about. A God who is a surprising God, a God who bothers about the one in 100, which is a statistic so easily discounted in our present society. God is also very un-shepherd-like, in that he doesn't send his servants to do the searching but goes after the sheep himself. This God is a searching God, a God who comes looking for us and who takes the initiative to find us. This God takes risks to do so and won't give up searching to bring us home to safety. And this God is a saving God, a God who wants to rescue us from danger and make sure we are safe from harm. He is also a God who is a shouldering God, a God who lifts us up to a place of safety, close to himself, and carries our burdens and takes the weight of our lost-ness on to himself. And finally this is a smiling God, a God who loves to celebrate you and me and share that joy with others.

Get ready

The following simple props might be helpful: a walking stick that looks like a crook; a toy sheepdog; a shawl to drape over your shoulders.

Get set

Perhaps the simplest way to tell this story is to relate it as a participative version of *We're Going on a Bear Hunt* by Michael Rosen (Margaret K. McElderry Books, 1989), only with sheep. You may find it helpful to have a copy of the book to hand.

Go!

As a way in, work with the first names of some of your audience. Repronounce these names, making the vowel reverberate like the sound of a sheep: e.g. Cha-a-a-rlie, Ja-a-ason, E-e-emily, Ma-a-asie.

Ask everyone to call out their new 'sheep name'.

Now you all sound like a herd of sheep! But what would happen if one of you went missing?

This is exactly what happened once to a shepherd looking after his flock of 100 sheep.

Ask if anyone has ever been lost and let each person tell a bit of their story briefly. Then ask who they think is possibly the most worried when someone is lost. Usually, it's not the person who is lost but the one who has lost someone. This opens up an insight into the story, where it is clear that it is the shepherd who gets most distressed about losing one of the sheep from his flock.

In the same way, God is the one who is really worried about us being lost, whereas we ourselves often don't realise there's a problem.

Jesus told this story...

Tell the story using the following obstacles: long wavy grass, a steep hill, a high fence, prickly thorn bushes, a deep river, a muddy meadow, a dark forest, sharp rocks, craggy boulders, creeping past dangerous animals and so on. Here's how to start:

> We're going on a sheep hunt!
> ***We're going on a sheep hunt!***
> We're going to find a lost one!
> ***We're going to find a lost one!***
> We're not scared!
> ***We're not scared!***
>
> Uh-oh!
> Grass!
> Long wavy grass.
> We can't go over it.
> We can't go under it.
> Oh no!
> We've got to go through it!
> Swishy swashy! Swishy swashy! Swishy swashy!
>
> Chorus: We're going on a sheep hunt... etc.

For each subsequent obstacle add appropriate actions. Until...

> Uh-oh!
> A cave!
> A deep dark cave.
> We can't go over it.
> We can't go under it.
> We've got to go through it!
> Tiptoe! Tiptoe! Tiptoe!

WHAT'S THAT?!
A shiny wet nose!
Two little ears!
A big woolly fleece
IT'S THE LOST SHEEP!
Hurray!
Let's go home to celebrate
Back through…

Prayer idea

For prayers, pick up on some of the actions in the story, namely:

Searching: invite everyone to shade their eyes and look all around the room.

Carrying: invite everyone to imagine holding a heavy sheep on their shoulders.

Celebration: on the count of three, invite everyone to punch the air with a great cheer.

Now use these three actions together and link them to three prayers that follow:

Thank you, Lord, that you came looking for us. Help us to be on the lookout for others who are in need of help in our communities.

Thank you, Lord, that you share our burdens and problems. Help us to follow that example and share the loads of those who are feeling overwhelmed by what they have to cope with.

Thank you, Lord, that you love us to be at home with you. Help us to show the world that you are a God who loves to celebrate and wants everyone to experience the joy of heaven right now on earth.

Amen

17
Messy market day

The parable of the sheep and the goats

When the Son of Man comes in his glory, and all the angels with him, he will sit on his glorious throne. All the nations will be gathered before him, and he will separate the people one from another as a shepherd separates the sheep from the goats. He will put the sheep on his right and the goats on his left.

Then the King will say to those on his right, 'Come, you who are blessed by my Father; take your inheritance, the kingdom prepared for you since the creation of the world. For I was hungry and you gave me something to eat, I was thirsty and you gave me something to drink, I was a stranger and you invited me in, I needed clothes and you clothed me, I was sick and you looked after me, I was in prison and you came to visit me.'

Then the righteous will answer him, 'Lord, when did we see you hungry and feed you, or thirsty and give you something to drink? When did we see you a stranger and invite you in, or needing clothes and clothe you? When did we see you sick or in prison and go to visit you?'

The King will reply, 'Truly I tell you, whatever you did for one of the least of these brothers and sisters of mine, you did for me.'

Then he will say to those on his left, 'Depart from me, you who are cursed, into the eternal fire prepared for the devil and his angels. For I was hungry and you gave me nothing to eat, I was thirsty and you gave me nothing to drink, I was a stranger and you did not invite me in, I needed clothes and you did not clothe me, I was sick and in prison and you did not look after me.'

They also will answer, 'Lord, when did we see you hungry or thirsty or a stranger or needing clothes or sick or in prison, and did not help you?'

He will reply, 'Truly I tell you, whatever you did not do for one of the least of these, you did not do for me.'

Then they will go away to eternal punishment, but the righteous to eternal life.

MATTHEW 25:31–46

Get ready

This is possibly the last parable Jesus told the crowds before his death on the cross. He wanted his hearers to know that judgement was coming and soon it would be time to sort out those whose faith in God had led them to care for others and those who had closed their hearts to God and also to people in need. He had already warned them about this great divide in his early parables of the wheat and the weeds and of the great catch of fish. When God looks on our lives, it won't be how clever we are, or what possessions we have, or how famous we have become that matters, but whether our faith in God was demonstrated in practical kindness towards our neighbour.

Jesus uses the dramatic imagery of a shepherd sorting out his goats and sheep on market day – a very familiar sight to those in that part of the world. The striking part of this parable is that those who showed kindness and love did so without realising it. Each little act of compassion is noticed by God and every time we care for others, it is also a way of loving God. Some commentators suggest that 'one of the least of these my brothers' refers just to Christians. However, as the parable is about the people of all nations before God's throne (v. 32), it is more likely that it means anybody who is in need – all who are part of God's creation. Everyone is our brother or sister and we can't say that we love God but ignore the needs of those around us in the human family.

Not showing love, it seems, is equally done without realising it, and the second group is condemned for not noticing people's needs. Indeed, how can anyone fail to see the massive needs there are in this world and not want do something to help? This is a challenging story for us all, but also a hopeful one, as it is clear that God does receive every little good thing we do as a way of serving him. And because God is always more ready to forgive than condemn, this is good news.

Finally, in a more direct way than yet recorded in Matthew's Gospel, Jesus makes it clear that he is the Son of Man who was prophesied – the story picks up messianic imagery from Daniel chapter 7; and also that he is God's Son, as he talks about 'my father'. He is making simply outrageous claims… unless they are true.

Get set

No special props are needed. It will help to have at least the last verse of the rewritten nursery rhyme (downloadable from **www.messychurch.org.uk/5504**) written out large for all to see so they can join in if they want to.

Go!

Invite everyone to make some sheep and goat sound effects ('baa-baa' and 'bleet-bleet'). Have some fun with this.

It must have been very noisy in the market place.

There were hundreds of sheep.

Invite sheep sound effects.

There were hundreds of goats.

Invite goat sound effects.

And they were all mixed up.

Invite a mixture of sounds.

But everyone knew that the sheep were more valuable to the shepherd, so they needed to be separated off. Sheep to the right!

Invite more sheep sound effects.

Goats to the left!

Invite more goat sound effects.

It must have been a messy, noisy business!

When Jesus saw this sort of thing happening in the markets of Capernaum, or perhaps out on the hills above Nazareth, it was a sight that stayed with him. He saw it as an important picture of what must happen one day.

He knew that, finally, at the end of time, there would have to be a separation between the good and the bad in this world. Things at the moment are not the way God intended. Things are all so noisy and messy.

But in all the noise, God knows which people are doing good things and which are doing bad things.

Even among those who trust in God and follow the way of Jesus, some are sadly doing bad things. And among those who have never even heard of God and who say they don't trust him, there are some who are doing good things.

One day it is going to be a very messy market day indeed. Only God can sort this out. And as each sheep or goat is brought before the Good Shepherd, he knows which sheep is truly sheep and which goat is truly goat.

Share the following as a confidential aside.

(You know, you can sometimes be sheep on the outside but goat on the inside; or you can be goat on the outside but sheep on the inside. This can sometimes even take the sheep and the goats by surprise!)

Sing the next bit to the traditional nursery rhyme tune of 'Baa baa black sheep':

Baa baa, black sheep, what good things… did you do?
Me sir, unsure sir, what did I do?
Did you care for the needy?
Welcome the alone?
Feed and clothe the poorest, and offer them a home?

Bleet bleet, black goat, what good things… did you do?
Me sir, unsure sir, what did I do?
Did you visit at the hospital?
Go to those in jail?
Did you share all your many things, with those beyond the pale?

Baa bleet, sheep and goats, what good things did you do?
Us sir, unsure sir, what should we do?
Care for the world I love
For all who have much less,
This is how to love the Lord, so you he will bless.

Jesus told this story of the great separation on market day.

Maybe this divide is inside all of us at the moment? Sheep and goat on the inside.

But how will it be in the end?

Which side will you be on when Jesus the Good Shepherd comes?

Invite everyone to join in with this last verse:

Baa bleet, sheep and goats, what good things did we do?
Us sir, unsure sir, what should we do?
Care for the world I love
For all who have much less,
This is how to love the Lord, so you he will bless.

Prayer idea

You will need a blow-up globe and Post-it notes.

The focus for this parable lends itself to prayers for any local initiatives of caring and social action and global aid issues.

For example, share news from a local food bank, ask for names of any known to your congregation who are unwell, bring in information about any charity work supported by your church and also mention any crisis or humanitarian need globally.

Write the names or causes on to Post-it notes, which you should stick on to a blow-up globe.

Lift up the globe as you pray over the situations named, ending with this verse from the story:

The King will reply, 'Truly I tell you, whatever you did for one of the least of these brothers and sisters of mine, you did for me.'

18 Messy motives

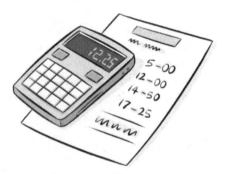

The parable of the shrewd manager

Jesus told his disciples: 'There was a rich man whose manager was accused of wasting his possessions. So he called him in and asked him, "What is this I hear about you? Give an account of your management, because you cannot be manager any longer."

'The manager said to himself, "What shall I do now? My master is taking away my job. I'm not strong enough to dig, and I'm ashamed to beg – I know what I'll do so that, when I lose my job here, people will welcome me into their houses."

'So he called in each one of his master's debtors. He asked the first, "How much do you owe my master?"

'"Nine hundred gallons of olive oil," he replied.

'The manager told him, "Take your bill, sit down quickly, and make it four hundred and fifty."

'Then he asked the second, "And how much do you owe?"

'"A thousand bushels of wheat," he replied.

'He told him, "Take your bill and make it eight hundred."

'The master commended the dishonest manager because he had acted shrewdly. For the people of this world are more shrewd in dealing with their own kind than are the people of the light. I tell you, use worldly wealth to gain friends for yourselves, so that when it is gone, you will be welcomed into eternal dwellings.'

LUKE 16:1–9

Get ready

Perhaps this should be entitled the parable of the rogue trader or the corrupt banker, as this may better express for us today the original shock impact that this parable would have had. The translation above describes the manager as 'shrewd', but the original Greek simply means sensible or even wise. So why is Jesus telling us a story where God, as represented by the rich man, commends a corrupt official? No wonder this parable's interpretation has caused commentators a few headaches.

And how does this parable connect with the other stories Luke records in this part of his Gospel? Is it about money, which indeed does become part of the focus for the conversation and stories that follow? Or is it about being lost, which the three parables before it address? It has been noted that the narrative returns to Jesus' original audience at verse 14, which is where it started before the stories of the lost sheep, coin and son; also that this corrupt manager 'wasted' or 'squandered' his employer's possessions, which is the exact same word that is used for the way the prodigal son behaved with his inheritance. Is this, therefore, another story about someone who is lost but who realises it in time and who at least does something about putting things right? The manager is praised for acting promptly and seizing the opportunity to make amends as best he could. His pragmatism is something to imitate because God welcomes people back home to himself, however they come and however messy their motives might be.

The surprise 'hero' of this story would really have upset Jesus' listeners, particularly the Pharisees. No wonder they mocked him when he told it (v. 14). However, this is typical of parables, which so often contain details that surprised and even outraged audiences, but with the intention of getting them to think again about the true nature of the kingdom of God. Often even 'the people of light' need shaking out of their blindness and complacency to see the truth properly. Even a rogue trader or corrupt banker might teach us a lesson sometimes.

Get set

You will need two piles of newspapers, preferably of different quality and size and including the *Financial Times*, which would fit well with this retelling of the story. This is how the story might have been told by Jesus to today's audience. You may find that having two voices to deliver this piece would work better for you.

Go!

Wave a newspaper taken from a pile, like a street vendor.

Scandal! Scandal! Big city scandal! Read all about it!

Trusted manager of huge corporation pockets millions of pounds for himself!

Address your audience as yourself now.

It's terrible. It's a disgrace! Corruption in the business place! It's typical! They say money is at the root of so many problems or, rather, the love of money. People never have enough.

Rogue traders… overpaid bankers… corrupt managers… they're all the same. They deserve all that's coming to them.

Pause. Pick up another paper from a different pile.

Scandal! Scandal! Big city scandal! Read all about!

Rogue trader reinstated. Huge corporation takes back untrustworthy manager!

Make as if you are reading the following from the paper.

'The manager at the centre of yesterday's financial scandal has been given his job back. It seems that before he was sacked, he did the firm some good by arranging for some large overseas debts to be repaid. He has helped put the company back on track and has improved their profit margins.'

Address the audience in shock.

Apparently the scoundrel's prompt action saved the corporation millions in unpaid bills. The man's come up smelling of roses!

Read again.

'"I knew I behaved badly as a manager and I deserved what was coming to me," he said to our reporter. "But I realised my mistake in time and decided to do something about it. I called in the firm's two biggest clients who owed large amounts of money. We did a deal securing repayment of a large part of their debt. The boss was pleased. I've learned my lesson and now I've got my job back!"'

Address the audience again.

The story is trending on Twitter and the press is divided in its opinion. What a turnaround. Does this man deserve to be punished or praised?

Read again.

'Late last night the firm's CEO gave this surprising statement. "The man's a genius. I won't have a bad word said against him. He is sensible and thoughtful. I like that in a manager."'

Address the audience again.

Social media is awash with comment. Mr Scoundrel or Mr Sensible?

What do you think?

That's the story that Jesus told, or at least in today's language.

It was a total turnaround. It was so unexpected.

Why was Jesus holding up the action of a man who was a thief as an example to follow? But then again, the man did at least do something when he faced up to his crimes. He took action rather than do nothing.

So what is Jesus saying?

Perhaps he is saying, '… and what about you? Will you be sensible when the time comes? Will you get ready to be part of the kingdom of God in time? Or will you leave it too late?'

That's what matters, however mixed your motives might be.

Prayer idea

Invite everybody to make four simple facial expressions that together summarise the story:

- a sad face – the manager is found out
- a thoughtful face – the manager thinks about what he should do
- a determined face – the manager gets on with sorting things out
- a happy face – the manager is back in the boss's good books

Use these, one with each of these four short prayers:

> **Sad face** – Lord God, I realise that I have not lived my life as you hoped.
> **Thoughtful face** – Lord God, thank you that you still love me but want me to change.
> **Determined face** – Lord God, I want to live differently and follow the way of Jesus.
> **Happy face** – Lord God, thank you that you are always ready to forgive and give me a new start.
> Amen

19

Messy riches

The parable of the man who built bigger barns

Someone in the crowd said [to Jesus], 'Teacher, tell my brother to divide the inheritance with me.'

Jesus replied, 'Man, who appointed me a judge or an arbiter between you?' Then he said to them, 'Watch out! Be on your guard against all kinds of greed; life does not consist in an abundance of possessions.'

And he told them this parable: 'The ground of a certain rich man yielded an abundant harvest. He thought to himself, "What shall I do? I have no place to store my crops."

'Then he said, "This is what I'll do. I will tear down my barns and build bigger ones, and there I will store my surplus grain. And I'll say to myself, 'You have plenty of grain laid up for many years. Take life easy; eat, drink and be merry.'"

'But God said to him, "You fool! This very night your life will be demanded from you. Then who will get what you have prepared for yourself?"

'This is how it will be with whoever stores up things for themselves but is not rich toward God.'

LUKE 12:13–21

Get ready

This parable is prompted by a family argument over an inheritance. The two brothers obviously thought that taking their quarrel to Jesus would resolve the matter, but they got more than they bargained for. Jesus rejects the role of judge in this case and instead tells them a story about the dangers of greed and selfishness.

In many ways this parable seems very straightforward. One way to sum it up could be with the saying, 'You can't take it with you when you go'. However, although most people may acknowledge that in their heads, in their hearts they still cling on to the importance of having a more than healthy bank balance. Money may not buy you love, but it can get you a lot in this life, though, as the rich farmer in this story clearly demonstrates, people never think they have enough. No wonder Paul warns his young apprentice Timothy in a letter that 'the love of money is the root of all evil'.

The shock of this parable for the audience at the time would have been that this rich man was a fool in God's eyes. Rich people were usually understood to be blessed by God. And, indeed, riches can be a blessing, but it is our heart's attitude to wealth that matters and this man is condemned for getting his priorities completely wrong. He never considers the poor or even anyone else, concerned only with his own future well-being.

This parable leads into teaching from Jesus about our attitude to possessions and the pointlessness of being preoccupied with worry. Of course, there are many in our world who do not have even the basics in this life and we should be worrying about them, caught up in this inequality. Sharing what we have with them is one way not to be 'poor in God's sight'; this is the way to true riches that this fool has neglected.

Get set

The following idea for retelling this parable is shaped by the familiar nursery rhyme format of 'This is the house that Jack built'. This could stand alone or be enhanced by assigning some simple actions to each new line of the story. For example:

- *Rich farmer* – rub fingers and thumb together on both hands to indicate wealth
- *Land* – describe a large upright rectangle with two hands
- *Seed* – pinch finger and thumb together as if holding a seed
- *Wheat* – gently wave one upright arm back and forth like a piece of wheat in the wind
- *Small barns* – make a building shape with two hands, the fingers linking to be the roof
- *Larger barns* – with your hands and arms describe the same shape as above in outline but larger
- *Massive barns* – with your hands and arms describe the same shape as above in outline but huge
- *Party* – wave hands about, dance and jig in party mood
- *Silence* – finger to mouth as for quiet

Go!

Money problems! We all have them!

Two brothers once had big money problems. They were rowing about how much each should inherit. They wanted Jesus to sort it out.

But Jesus wasn't getting involved. And anyway, they had got their priorities all wrong. Instead, Jesus told them a story.

Teach the actions suggested above and add these in for the key words.

This is the *rich farmer* who owned lots of *land*.

This is the **seed** that belonged to the **rich farmer**, who owned lots of **land**.

This is the harvest of **wheat**, grown from the **seed** that belonged to the **rich farmer**, who owned lots of **land**.

These are the **small barns** that tried to store the harvest of **wheat**, grown from the **seed** that belonged to the **rich farmer**, who owned lots of **land**.

These are the **larger barns**, built instead of the **small barns** that tried to store the harvest of **wheat**, grown from the **seed** that belonged to the **rich farmer**, who owned lots of **land**.

And these are the truly **massive barns**, put up to take the place of the **larger barns**, built instead of the **small barns** that tried to store the harvest of **wheat**, grown from the **seed** that belonged to the **rich farmer**, who owned lots of **land**.

This is the sound of the all-night **party** in the big house, not far from the truly **massive barns**, put up to take the place of the **larger barns**, built instead of the **small barns** that tried to store the harvest of **wheat**, grown from the **seed** that belonged to the **rich farmer**, who owned lots of **land**.

But this is the sound of the **silence**… after death interrupted the sound of the all-night **party** in the big house, not far from the truly **massive barns**, put up to take the place of the **larger barns**, built instead of the **small barns** that tried to store the harvest of **wheat**, grown from the **seed** that belonged to the **rich farmer**, who owned lots of **land**…

…. and who had died, having forgotten that the most important thing in life was to be rich in the sight of God.

Pause.

I wonder, what is it that makes us rich in God's sight?

What makes us poor?

What can we do about it?

Prayer idea

Like it or not, from the perspective of most, we in the developed nations are the rich man in this story.

Use this prayer space as an opportunity to focus on the work of a mission or aid agency supported by your church. Share a particular up-to-the-minute need and encourage everyone to think how they could respond. Rather than build bigger barns, how might we help those in need at least have some seed of their own to plant?

Use a prayer suggested by a mission or aid agency prayer diary, or alternatively this more general prayer:

> Lord God, help us to use the riches you have given us wisely
> and may they not blind us to the needs of others.
> Amen

20 Messy seeds

The parable of the mustard seed

[Jesus] told them another parable: 'The kingdom of heaven is like a mustard seed, which a man took and planted in his field. Though it is the smallest of all seeds, yet when it grows, it is the largest of garden plants and becomes a tree, so that the birds come and perch in its branches.'

MATTHEW 13:31–32 (see also MARK 4:30–32 and LUKE 13:18–19)

Get ready

It's just two verses long but each of the synoptic Gospels records this tiny parable. It must have been a popular one among the disciples, perhaps because it was so short, but also because it was surprising and mysterious. Just how is God's kingdom like a mustard seed that grows into a tree? And what do the birds of the air represent? The birds in the parable of the sower, according to Jesus, stand for the devil, but surely that can't be right here.

Once again, parables are deceptively simple stories with surprises around every corner. It also doesn't help to know that the sort of small tree that this mustard seed became was regarded as a nuisance by most gardeners in Palestine – a sort of mini Leylandii tree in the wrong place. So what is that saying about God's kingdom?

The contrast between the tiny seed and the tree it becomes is at the heart of this story. God's kingdom may have small beginnings but this parable encourages his disciples to know that it will grow and indeed is growing. In another saying of Jesus, he says that even a mustard seed of faith can move mountains, and in the Old Testament scriptures, God tells his people never to 'despise the day of small beginnings' (Zechariah 4:10).

Even so, this is a strange tale. The tree images familiar to his audience, found in the books of Ezekiel (chapter 17) and Daniel (chapter 4) and which represented huge empires, were grand botanical specimens like the cedars of Lebanon and not an over-large vegetable plant such as a mustard tree. It would have amused his listeners to compare God's kingdom to this. Here is the humour that Jesus often used to surprise people and subvert their thinking. And what about the birds, usually a pest for a gardener – certainly at sowing time? They come from all points of the compass, so maybe they stand for non-Jews – outsiders like the Greeks and Romans, who had invaded their promised land over the centuries. What is Jesus suggesting? His audience hated the pagan Romans and Greeks. Who will be in God's kingdom? From the perspective of today, however, we can look back and see how this parable has been fulfilled.

Get set

No special props are needed to tell this story.

Go!

Jesus often answered questions with more questions and even seems to have enjoyed speaking in riddles.

Here are some examples (all below are from the CEV):

- 'The people of this world won't be able to see me, but you will see me.' (John 14:19)
- 'If you love your life, you will lose it.' (John 12:25)
- 'No one who drinks the water I give will ever be thirsty again.' (John 4:14)
- 'Everyone who is now first will be last, and everyone who is last will be first.' (Matthew 20:16)

Try these popular riddles out on your Messy congregation:

I sit on a bridge. Some people will look through me while others wonder what I hide. What am I?

(Answer: Sunglasses. They sit on the bridge of your nose, you look through them but other people wonder what they hide.)

What falls, but never breaks? What breaks, but never falls?

(Answer: Day and night.)

Four fingers and a thumb yet flesh and bone I have none, what am I?

(Answer: A glove.)

Now try this one. It is linked to today's story:

I start my life out of sight;
Hidden in dark, I move towards light;
I am as much below as I am above;
To reach my best, I need lots of love;
I was so tiny, but now reach high;
A place for birds up in the sky.
I am in the Bible – what am I?

(Answer: A mustard seed that becomes a tree.)

Now tell the parable using your hands, inviting everyone to copy your actions. Tell it slowly.

Jesus once told this story. He said God's kingdom… is like a seed.

Hold finger and thumb together as if a tiny seed is caught between the two.

The tiniest of seeds. A small mustard seed.

Place the imaginary seed on the palm of your hand and look at it, amazed at its smallness.

So small that even the birds of the air would fly past without noticing it. And even if they did, it was too small to bother eating.

Turn the other hand into a bird flying past for whom the seed is so small it doesn't even notice it.

The farmer took the tiny mustard seed and planted it in the soil.

Push the seed deep into your palm as if planting it.

The seed went down into the dark earth where it could grow in secret.

Wrap your fist around the imaginary seed as if this is now under the ground.

The days and weeks passed. The sun shone and the rain fell. The sun shone and the rain fell.

Use the other hand to represent the sunshine beaming down and the rain pouring down.

Time passed and slowly the little seed began to push its first shoots above the surface.

Make one finger begin to move upwards from the fist like the first tiny shoot from the seed plant.

The shoot became bigger. The bigger shoot became a plant.

Move the finger so it slowly 'grows' taller.

The plant became a small shrub. The small shrub became a bigger shrub. The big shrub grew branches, which themselves grew and…

And make it taller using more and more of your hand to imitate becoming a tiny shrub… a bigger shrub… and eventually…

It became a small tree, which became a big tree.

Use the whole hand and arm, slowly stretching the fingers out wide to be branches and a big tree.

Such a big tree that the birds of the air flew from all over…

Use the other hand now to represent a bird again flying towards the tree. This time it does see the tree, not as something to eat but as somewhere to shelter.

And they made their nests in its branches.

Have your 'hand' bird sit between the fingers of the 'tree' hand.

Pause.

That's what God's kingdom is like, said Jesus.

Pause again.

What did he mean?

What was he saying?

How is a tree like God's kingdom? It's not even a very beautiful tree!

And what are the birds meant to be?

And where is the seed now?

Just what is Jesus telling us?

Prayer idea

Teach this simple response for the prayers, perhaps linking it with the hand pictures for 'seed' and 'tree' in the story above.

With God small can be big and a little can go a long way.

Thank you, Lord, that you only need a little faith to bring your love into our lives.
With God small can be big and a little can go a long way.

Thank you, Lord, that you only need a little love from us for you to multiply it to those around us.
With God small can be big and a little can go a long way.

Thank you, Lord, that you only need a little 'yes' from us for you to make our lives into a channel of your peace.
With God small can be big and a little can go a long way.

Thank you, Lord, that you see the people who feel small and unimportant and you care about each becoming the best they can be.
With God small can be big and a little can go a long way.
Amen

21
Messy soils

The parable of the sower

Jesus said: 'Listen! A farmer went out to plant his seed. He scattered the seed on the ground. Some fell on a path. Birds came and ate it up. Some seed fell on rocky places, where there wasn't much soil. The plants came up quickly, because the soil wasn't deep. When the sun came up, it burned the plants. They dried up because they had no roots. Other seed fell among thorns. The thorns grew up and crowded out the plants. So the plants did not bear grain. Still other seed fell on good soil. It grew up and produced a crop 30, 60, or even 100 times more than the farmer planted.'

MARK 4:3–8 (see also MATTHEW 13:1–9 and LUKE 8:4–8)

Get ready

This well-known parable is found in Matthew, Mark and Luke's Gospels along with an explanation of its meaning from Jesus. It was clearly a well-remembered and popular story that Jesus quite probably used on more than one occasion. You can easily imagine the crowds calling out, 'Tell us the one about the farmer sowing seed,' just like young children asking for their favourite story again and again. The version in each of the three Gospels is almost identical. It was clearly often told by the first Christians, just as it still is today.

This and the parable of the wheat and the weeds are the only two parables recorded where we also have Jesus' private explanation of their meaning given to his disciples. Both come early on in the records of Jesus' preaching and serve as an example both of the sort of parables he used and of the way in which we have to work hard to uncover the meaning of all his subsequent parables. In this sense, it is a parable about parables, as well as containing its own surprising insights about the kingdom of God.

In Matthew, Mark and Luke's Gospels this parable is linked to a short section with a quotation from the book of Isaiah that explains why Jesus used stories in the way he did. His stories seemed simple enough, but they had hidden depths that were intended to stimulate the listeners to work out the meaning for themselves. As Jesus says: God has given you a pair of ears, so use them (my version of Mark 4:9). Jesus may have been easy to listen to, but it took effort to understand.

A better title for this parable would be 'the parable of the soils'. Although the explanation of the story talks about the seed, it is the people who hear, represented by the different types of soil, that are the focus. It must have helped the disciples understand why some people didn't respond to Jesus as they had done; some hearts were simply too hard, some too shallow and some too distracted. The big surprise of this parable comes at the end. An average harvest in first-century Palestine would have yielded a seven or eight per cent return on the sowing; this harvest brings in a staggering 30, 60 or 100 per cent return. Where God is at work in a human heart amazing things can happen.

The following retelling endeavours simply to enable your Messy congregation to encounter the story – indeed it may even be a story they have never heard before. It leaves them the job of working out its meaning for themselves. Is it about anyone who hears the good news about Jesus or is it particularly about those who become his followers? Is Jesus saying that some may start off as disciples but will then abandon the faith? Or is it about both?

Get set

There are no particular props for this retelling, but it will work best if you try and learn it as best you can beforehand so you don't have to keep referring to a script. What happens to each of the seeds also lends itself to easy participation from the audience with actions and sounds for being gobbled up, withering away, being choked and growing successfully. And as your audience becomes familiar with the lines and the pattern of the story, encourage them to join in.

Go!

Jesus loved telling stories.

He was such a good storyteller.

And people loved listening to his stories.

'Tell us the one about the sheep,' they would cry. 'Let's hear the one about the coins again,' they'd call out.

Or, 'We want the one about the farmer sowing seed.'

Listen, said Jesus. You need to listen carefully. There's always more to my stories than meets the ear.

So are you are ready?

Are you all ears?

Are you ready to listen hard?

OK, let's go.

The following story uses the nursery rhyme pattern of 'One man went to mow'.

A farmer went to sow, went to sow his meadow. A farmer and his seed… went to sow his meadow.

The farmer scattered seed, some fell upon the hard soil.
First seed, hard soil; sown seed... he went to sow his meadow.

Some birds came flying down, ate up all the first seed.
Gobbled up, first seed, hard soil; sown seed... he went to sow
his meadow.

The farmer scattered seed, some fell upon the thin soil.
Second seed, thin soil; gobbled up, first seed, hard soil; sown
seed... he went to sow his meadow.

This seed tried to grow, but had no room for rooting.
Dried up, second seed, thin soil; gobbled up, first seed, hard
soil; sown seed... he went to sow his meadow.

The farmer scattered seed, some fell among the sharp thorns.
Third seed, thorny soil; dried up, second seed, thin soil;
gobbled up, first seed, hard soil; sown seed... he went to sow
his meadow.

The thorns grew thick and fast, strangled them to pieces.
Strangled, third seed, thorny soil; dried up, second seed, thin
soil; gobbled up, first seed, hard soil; sown seed... he went to
sow his meadow.

The farmer scattered seed, some fell upon the good soil.
Fourth seed, good soil; strangled, third seed, thorny soil; dried
up, second seed, thin soil; gobbled up, first seed, hard soil;
sown seed... he went to sow his meadow.

*Slow the pace of the retelling to emphasise what happened to the last
group of seeds.*

The last seeds began to grow, they produced a MASSIVE
harvest.

Say the next part as fast as you can.

> Massive harvest, fourth seed, good soil; strangled, third seed, thorny soil; dried up, second seed, thin soil; gobbled up, first seed, hard soil; sown seed…

Make a dramatic pause and catch your breath for a slow triumphant last line.

> He went to sow his meadow!

What a story!

But did you listen?

Did you hear?

I wonder what it all means.

Jesus said there was much more to this story than meets the ear.

What was he talking about?

Prayer idea

You will need some packets of seeds (not too small and that are safe to eat, such as sunflower seeds).

Hand out the seeds and invite them to hold their seeds in the different ways described below and use the words suggested for each position.

Holding the seed in the palm of the hand:

> This seed is special. It contains life waiting to break out. It is precious and valuable. It is a gift from God. Like this seed, each of our lives is precious and special. God has given each of us a life that is beyond price.

Forgive us, Lord, for taking the gift of life for granted and for not treating each other as your precious children.

Holding up the seed between finger and thumb:

This seed is small. It seems too tiny to be anything important or significant. Yet it contains a surprise waiting to happen. It is a lesson from God. Like this seed, God planned each of our lives to become something surprisingly more than we yet are or appear to be.

Forgive us, Lord, for not recognising the small beginnings of your work in us and for not believing in your surprising plans for our lives.

Holding the seed hidden in the closed fist of one hand:

This seed is hidden. It remains out of sight so it can grow in secret. The miracle of the seed can only happen as it dies in the depth of the earth. It is a sign from God. Like this seed, God wants us to be with him in secret. He wants to work in depth in our lives. We can only grow as we trust in the miracle of his new life out of death.

Forgive us, Lord, for not spending time with you and for tolerating those things in us that ought to be put to death.

Place the seed on a surface in front of you and pause to consider what this seed will become one day.

Pause.

May we grow up to become the best we can. Thank you for promising us all a new beginning through what happened to Jesus on the cross.
Amen

22
Messy tenants

The parable of the tenants and the vineyard

Listen to another parable: There was a landowner who planted a vineyard. He put a wall around it, dug a winepress in it and built a watchtower. Then he rented the vineyard to some farmers and moved to another place. When the harvest time approached, he sent his servants to the tenants to collect his fruit.

The tenants seized his servants; they beat one, killed another, and stoned a third. Then he sent other servants to them, more than the first time, and the tenants treated them the same way. Last of all, he sent his son to them. 'They will respect my son,' he said.

But when the tenants saw the son, they said to each other, 'This is the heir. Come, let's kill him and take his inheritance.' So they took him and threw him out of the vineyard and killed him.

Therefore, when the owner of the vineyard comes, what will he do to those tenants?

'He will bring those wretches to a wretched end,' they replied, 'and he will rent the vineyard to other tenants, who will give him his share of the crop at harvest time.'

Jesus said to them, 'Have you never read in the Scriptures: "The stone the builders rejected has become the cornerstone; the Lord has done this, and it is marvellous in our eyes"? Therefore I tell you that the kingdom of God will be taken away from you and given to a people who will produce its fruit. Anyone who falls on this stone will be broken to pieces; anyone on whom it falls will be crushed.'

When the chief priests and the Pharisees heard Jesus' parables, they knew he was talking about them. They looked for a way to arrest him, but they were afraid of the crowd because the people held that he was a prophet.

MATTHEW 21:33–46 (see also MARK 12:1–12 and LUKE 20:9–19)

Get ready

Three Gospel writers agree that this powerful parable comes near the end of Jesus' ministry and was most probably told in Holy Week. It is also the parable that finally seems to have tipped the balance as far as the religious authorities were concerned. A man who talked like this was blasphemous and should die.

Personally, I find this by far the most moving and impactful of all the parables. Here, only thinly disguised, is the whole story of God's dealings with his people, including the coming of Jesus and a clear prediction of his death. In fact, it couldn't be clearer for those who had ears to hear, and some of the priests and Pharisees clearly understood what he meant.

Absentee landowners weren't uncommon in first-century Palestine, running their estates from outside the country through tenant farmers and expecting the rent in kind at harvest time. It took up to four years for a vineyard to be established as commercially productive, so it was no wonder that the tenants in the parable felt that it should all belong to them – after all, they were doing all the hard work. The sympathies of Jesus' audience at the time would have been with the tenants until, that is, they began to act so cruelly and finally they killed the owner's son. This is the twist in the tale that would have stunned them.

Jesus draws on familiar imagery for his Jewish audience. The vineyard was a well-established symbol of the nation of Israel – a huge golden vine hung over the entrance to the sanctuary in the temple – and there was also Isaiah's well-known parable of the vineyard in chapter 5 of his prophecy. However, Jesus takes something old and adds something new, just as he recommended a good storyteller should in his commentary on parables in Matthew 13. He adds the servants who come for the harvest on the owner's behalf and also, devastatingly, the coming of the owner's son with his terrible fate. Surely Jesus told this story with huge sorrow in his heart.

Another new thing that Jesus introduces is the link to the prophecy of 'the stone that the builders rejected' found in Psalm 118. Rather than interpreting this as a reference to the rejection of Israel as a nation into exile and then its restoration, he asks his audience to rethink its meaning. Jesus will be rejected but later restored to the highest place – in other words, here is a prophecy of his resurrection.

It is quite possible that a number of stones lay around the outskirts of the temple; stones that had been rejected by the builders. Herod's temple took a long time to build and it was most likely still being finished in Jesus' own time. Maybe it was a rejected stone that prompted this very parable, and this is the thought that shapes the storytelling suggestion below.

Get set

You will need a basket of reasonably sized, similar-looking stones from a garden centre and also one much larger single stone. The stones become the prompt for, and help tell, this story. You will also need some grapes for the prayer.

Go!

Many strange things happened during the last week of Jesus' life. Jesus and his friends stayed in a village outside the city near to a hill called the Mount of Olives. Each morning he would go into town and join with the festival crowds; and then near the temple he would sit down and tell stories.

The temple was a magnificent building. It had taken years and years to build. It shone with its golden decorations; its beautiful carved stonework gleamed in the sunlight; its towers and columns were overpowering in their splendour. But this temple was still being worked on. There was still building in progress and so there were some stones lying around that the builders had rejected. It was near these once that Jesus told a very special story.

Pick up and consider some of the small stones first.

Just think how old these stones might be. How far have they come? They have been cut from quarries, chipped and shaped to become parts of this magnificent temple. Of course, not every stone brought had been used. And there was one large stone in particular that caught Jesus' eye.

Draw everyone's attention to the big stone – feel its shape as the story begins to unfold.

This is one of the stones that the builders have rejected. I wonder what they didn't like about it. I wonder why they decided they couldn't use it. Is it the wrong shape, perhaps? Wouldn't it fit? Didn't they like its colour?

Then Jesus went on to say that it made him think of a song from the Psalms.

Look up and imagine you are like Jesus remembering words he learned when he was very young.

'The stone the builders rejected has become the most important stone of all. This is something that God has done – something amazing for us all.'

Now use the smaller stones to help tell the parable as indicated.

Then Jesus told this story to show them what he meant:

There was once a landowner who planted a vineyard. He wanted grapes to grow so he could make some fine wine.

He called in the builders to make a strong wall right around his land to keep the vineyard safe.

Make a wall around an open space with some of the stones.

He got his men to dig a ditch to keep out the wild animals.

He even prepared a great vat in which they could collect the grapes once they'd grown, to crush them for the juice to make the wine.

This was his own vineyard – his special place.

Finally he had one more building put up. On the edge of the vineyard he built a great tower – a watchtower to make sure no enemies came to steal the grapes.

Build a small tower with the remaining stones at one corner.

He did everything possible to make sure of a perfect harvest.

But then the landowner had to go on a journey. So he left some hired servants to look after the vineyard in his absence. But he was away longer than he planned – he couldn't be there when harvest came.

So he sent some messengers to go and bring back a share of the harvest so he could at least taste the fine grapes that he had planted.

When those messengers came, the hired servants decided that they would not give up what they'd been looking after. They wanted the vineyard for themselves. Instead of giving the messengers some of the harvest, they told them to push off. They beat them up, chased them away and sent them packing.

Mime some actions for what the servants did.

When the owner got to hear what was happening, he sent some more messengers, but they too were badly treated. They even killed some and threw stones at others, so that none dared go near the vineyard. Every group that the owner sent was treated in the same terrible way.

Mime some actions for what the servants did.

Finally the owner decided to send his own son to the vineyard. They won't dare treat him badly, he thought. They will respect him. They will hand over some of the grapes to him so he can bring them back to me.

When the hired servants saw the son coming, they began to plot. This is the owner's son, they thought. It will all be his one day. But, if we get rid of him, then the vineyard could truly be ours. So they ganged up on him. They grabbed him. They dragged him outside the vineyard and... they killed him.

Bring one of the small rocks crashing down on to the big rock to indicate the moment of the son's death.

The crowds near Jesus drew a sharp intake of breath. What a terrible story; and even as they were thinking that, Jesus asked this question:

What do you think the owner will do next?

Invite some responses from the congregation.

You're right. They deserve death. The vineyard doesn't belong to the likes of them.

They have rejected the owner's only son. But listen...

Slowly lift the big stone.

The one that was rejected will become the most important one.

The one that was tossed aside will become the one that holds everything together.

Only God can do this and it will be amazing.

I wonder what Jesus was talking about?

What's this got to do with what happened to Jesus?

Many in the crowd were puzzled, but some of them realised that the story was partly about them and they were angry.

Prayer idea

In the story the vineyard owner never got to taste his own harvest of grapes.

Distribute some small bunches of grapes amongst your Messy congregation.

Jesus was the stone that was rejected on the cross, but he became the most important stone of all, which the world recognised after his resurrection.

Because of this, we can come home to God and begin to taste the goodness of heaven right now.

Eat and enjoy the grapes and invite everyone to share in this prayer.

Thank you, Lord Jesus, that you were rejected in my place, but that now you are alive and we can come home to Father God through you.
Amen

23
Messy travellers

The parable of the good Samaritan

In reply Jesus said: 'A man was going down from Jerusalem to Jericho when he was attacked by robbers. They stripped him of his clothes, beat him and went away, leaving him half-dead. A priest happened to be going down the same road, and when he saw the man, he passed by on the other side. So too, a Levite, when he came to the place and saw him, passed by on the other side. But a Samaritan, as he travelled, came where the man was; and when he saw him, he took pity on him. He went to him and bandaged his wounds, pouring on oil and wine. Then he put the man on his own donkey, brought him to an inn and took care of him. The next day he took out two denarii and gave them to the innkeeper. "Look after him," he said, "and when I return, I will reimburse you for any extra expense you may have."

'Which of these three do you think was a neighbour to the man who fell into the hands of robbers?'

The expert in the law replied, 'The one who had mercy on him.'

Jesus told him, 'Go and do likewise.'

LUKE 10:30–37

Get ready

This parable comes during a conversation with a religious expert who had wanted to know what he should do to be sure of getting to heaven. As he so often did, Jesus returns the question to the questioner, knowing in this case that the expert already knew the answer and that he was just testing him. The expert quotes the Shema from Deuteronomy 6 as the most important instruction from God, namely to love God with all our being and to love our neighbour. However, in order not to lose face, the expert then asked a question about the definition of the word 'neighbour', and this is the story Jesus tells him as a reply.

This is such a well-known story for most of us that we can so easily miss the shock value for the lawyer and those listening. Today the term 'good Samaritan' has become shorthand for someone who steps up to the mark to help others in need; it is part of our everyday language. There is also the Samaritans charity, who are there on the phone for those in crisis. However, the Samaritans in Jesus' day were a mixed-race community who had, according to true Jews, forfeited their right to be Jewish at the time of the exile. They had devised their own form of Judaism, including their own temple and priestly system. True Jews prayed against them and avoided going through Samaria – although notably Jesus didn't do that and even stopped to talk with a Samaritan woman, thus breaching two great taboos. In short, the two groups hated one another. In order to capture the original impact of this parable in a modern version, you would have to substitute something like a 'foreign terrorist' for the word Samaritan; that's how shocking it would have sounded.

The other surprising part of this story for those listening would have been the fact that it was two respected religious leaders who failed to show compassion for their fellow Jew, who had been brutally mugged. When it comes to compassion for those in need, Jesus is saying that you are more likely to find it in a despised outsider than within the family of faith. Naturally, this would have outraged most of his listeners. But unless our love for God is worked out in the real world of responding to those who ask for help, then that love is empty. Perhaps we find this most clearly expressed in the New Testament in John's first letter (1 John 4:20–21): 'Whoever claims to love God yet hates a brother or sister is a liar. For whoever does not love their brother and sister, whom they have seen, cannot love God, whom they have not seen. And he has given us this command: anyone who loves God must also love their brother and sister.'

The steep downhill road from Jerusalem to Jericho was notorious for violent robbery – it was even known as 'the red road' because so much blood had been spilled there. It was foolish for people to risk travelling alone, which is another reason this story would have caught everyone's attention. However, this isn't what Jesus focuses on. Nor does he offer any comment on the fact that the priest and Levite don't stop. It is who shows compassion that matters.

The final aspect of the story that is sometimes overlooked is that the victim has to learn a life-changing lesson. All his instincts as a Jew would have been to recoil from being helped by a hated foreigner, but he had to learn to receive compassion and love from this outsider. This can sometimes be as challenging for us as having pity on our neighbour.

Get set

There are no particular props needed for this storytelling. The idea is to encourage some impromptu mime from groups in the congregation to support your narrative. If you are enthusiastic and join in too, then it will work. Encourage mixed-age or family groups to come up and help you tell the story with as much drama and fun as possible. Every time an action is described (in bold below), invite the groups you called up to mime that action, such as 'carrying a heavy suitcase' or 'walking carefully down the road'.

Go!

Once someone asked Jesus what God would say is the best way to live. He already knew the answer, but was just testing Jesus.

Jesus got him to quote the Bible where it says it is 'to love God with all your heart, mind, soul and strength; and to love our neighbour as ourselves'.

The questioner wanted to push Jesus into saying more, so he asked again, 'But what does the Bible mean by "neighbour"? Is it just the person next door?'

Jesus then told this story.

Invite a group up to help you mime the first part of the parable.

Once a man was travelling from a big city to a small city. **He reached up high** to collect his big suitcase from on top of the wardrobe and **began packing** for his journey. He put in all sorts of things.

Ask for suggestions from the congregation as the group mime 'filling up the suitcase'.

He then **tried to close the suitcase**, but it was too full. **He pushed and shoved; he jumped on it, sat on it**. But it was no good. He had to **remove some of the items**. He eventually **managed to close the suitcase**. Now, this wasn't one with wheels, so he had to carry it in the old-fashioned way. He **picked up his heavy suitcase, staggering with its weight** as he **waved goodbye** to his family and his friends in Jerusalem, which was the big city, to set out on the journey south to Jericho, the small city.

Change your group for a different one to continue with the mime interpretation of your story.

The road down to Jericho wasn't an easy one. There were **rocks to avoid, potholes to walk around and even donkey poo to step over**. On top of that, **the suitcase was heavy** and the road was downhill, so **he had to proceed slowly**. The road became more and more lonely and the rocks either side looked more and more menacing. The man with the suitcase was now **walking very nervously indeed**.

Change your group again.

This was a well-known road for **robbers lurking behind the rocks** who were **looking out for a lone traveller** coming down the road. In the distance **they caught sight** of a traveller with a fat suitcase getting closer and closer. They **poised themselves ready for the attack**; then they **leapt out, punching, kicking, grabbing all they could from the poor traveller, taking his posh clothes, his suitcase and giving him a final big kick before they ran and ran as fast as they could**.

Change your group again.

Look at the poor traveller lying by the road half-dead and with everything taken from him. He needs help.

Just then **another traveller came down the road**. He was a priest in the temple in Jerusalem and was **reading from his scroll** as he walked, thinking about the great law of God; about loving God with all his heart, mind, soul and strength, and your neighbour as yourself. He was going to give a sermon about it in the synagogue down in Jericho. When **suddenly he spotted the poor man** lying half-dead in a pool of blood by the side of the road, needing help. The priest daren't touch the blood and **he was scared as he looked around**. Maybe there were other robbers waiting to come and attack him. **He thought about what to do**. He knew what to do, but instead **he ran away as fast as he could**.

Change your group again.

Some time later **another traveller came down the road**. This man also worked in the temple and was a musician **practising his favourite instrument**. He helped lead the singing in the temple and **he was humming to himself** as he worked out a song that might tell the story about how we should love God with all our heart and strength, and our neighbour as ourselves. When suddenly **he too spotted the victim** beside the road, lying half-dead and desperately in need of help and in an even bigger pool of blood. This was someone from Jerusalem; someone he knew; someone who used to worship in the temple. **He thought about what he should do**. He knew what he should do. But maybe this was a trap. 'If I stop to help, they'll get me too.' He **thought about it again**, but not much before **he ran away as fast as he could.**

Change your group again.

Finally, a **third traveller came down the road**. This man **had a big smile on his face**. He was so glad to be away from Jerusalem. He hated Jerusalem and its people. He came from a place called Samaria, where he believed the true Jews were. He didn't even talk to people from Jerusalem. He was so happy as **he led his donkey along the road** to Jericho. Then **he spotted the man** who had been beaten up, left half-dead and who was in desperate need of help. He could see this man was from Jerusalem; someone he would never normally talk to, let alone touch. And someone who would never talk to him. **He thought about it** but then **he had pity on the victim, got on his knees to help, washed the man's wounds with oil, put his own coat on him, lifted him up onto the donkey and led the donkey and the man down the road to the nearest small hotel. He paid for a room for the night and stayed with him, caring for him** and the next morning **he gave the hotel manager enough money for more days of caring** and promised to come back if more money were needed. Then **he went on his way to Jericho**.

When Jesus finished this story, the crowd was silent and shocked, amazed by the characters Jesus had chosen. The two religious people hadn't helped, but the Samaritan, who they all hated, had shown compassion.

Jesus then turned to the man who had asked the question and said, 'Which of these was a true neighbour to the man who needed help?'

It was obvious what the answer was but at first no one dared say.

What was Jesus telling them? What was he saying about loving God and loving our neighbour?

Embarrassed, the man mumbled, 'The one who showed compassion.'

Jesus then turned and said, 'Go and do the same as that Samaritan.'

For some that was perhaps the hardest part of the whole story to hear. What do you think?

Prayer idea

It has been said that the robbers' attitude was, 'What's yours is mine and I'm taking it'; the religious travellers' attitudes were, 'What's mine is mine and I'm keeping it'; but the Samaritan's was, 'What's mine is yours and I'm sharing it'.

With three simple actions using both hands, for grabbing, hoarding and sharing, link them to these three prayers:

Grabbing action – We are sorry that we have taken from others thoughtlessly.
Hoarding action – Forgive us for holding on to what you have given us selfishly.
Sharing action – Help us to love you and love our neighbour by sharing all we have generously.
Amen

24
Messy treasures

The parable of the hidden treasure and the pearl

[Jesus said,] 'The kingdom of heaven is like treasure hidden in a field. When a man found it, he hid it again, and then in his joy went and sold all he had and bought that field.

'Again, the kingdom of heaven is like a merchant looking for fine pearls. When he found one of great value, he went away and sold everything he had and bought it.'

MATTHEW 13:44–46

Get ready

These two short parables belong together. They share the same truth but are told for two different audiences. The first might be farmers who knew about digging in fields, while the second might be businessmen, particularly those interested in fine jewels. Jesus knew how to tell stories that would catch the attention of different sorts of people.

Whether it was a farmer coming across riches by accident while digging, or a merchant intentionally on the lookout for the perfect pearl, once they find the treasure, there is no stopping them; they do everything possible to make sure that this treasure is theirs. Jesus offers no comment or explanation for either of the two parables but leaves it up to his audience to work out what they might mean. Maybe his disciples asked Jesus later, as they had done about the parable of the sower, but if they did, there is no record of his reply.

It was not unusual that someone might have buried his family fortune in the ground. There were banks in Jesus' day, but most people just hid their money somewhere safe. Also, according to Jewish law it was 'finders keepers', though owning the land would have made even that more secure. Pearls from the Far East often passed through Palestine on their way to markets in the cities of the Roman Empire. Alert traders used to be on the lookout for new and particularly fine specimens to add to their collection. The idea, though, that one merchant might sell everything he owned to buy one pearl is really hard to believe, but it is part of Jesus' storytelling style that made people both laugh and sit up and think.

Both the buried treasure and the precious pearl are, according to the beginning of each parable, clues to the kingdom of heaven. Whether we search for or merely stumble across the truth about heaven, God and eternal life, these stories suggest that we shouldn't let that truth out of our sight. Nothing should get in the way of holding on to it for ever. The search for 'the meaning of life, the universe and everything' has often been the subject matter of both serious and comic literature, as well as much philosophical debate. Jesus is saying that this is indeed the most important thing to talk about and it brings us home to God, but it is also something that in the end we must find for ourselves. These parables make it clear that finding the kingdom of heaven is the best thing that can happen to anyone. It is a treasure worth putting everything else aside for. As the missionary martyr Jim Elliot once wrote: 'He is no fool who gives what he cannot keep to gain what he cannot lose.'

Get set

What follows is a simple storyteller's version of these two parables. It doesn't rely on any clever techniques, imagery or visual aids, but offers a way to retell the stories so that hopefully they retain something of the impact they had when Jesus first told them.

Go!

Just imagine, said Jesus once, just imagine that you were out on a hillside digging away and suddenly your spade hit something metallic. There's something under the ground. You dig a bit further and discover the top of a box – a treasure chest. With excitement you work away to free the lid and there inside there is… a hoard of gold!

The trouble is, said Jesus, this treasure is buried in open land. It belongs to no one… yet. And if you carry on, people might notice and come over. You want to make this treasure yours. So, what do you do? Well, of course, you do everything possible to make sure that this land belongs to you. You won't want to share the treasure with anyone else or risk someone else finding it.

So you cover it up, rush off and sell up whatever you have to, to get the cash to buy that piece of land.

Just imagine, said Jesus, just imagine working in a jeweller's shop. You are an expert jeweller. You know everything about rubies, diamonds and especially pearls. And always, always, you are hoping to find the perfect pearl; the most beautiful pearl in the world.

And one day, said Jesus, one day someone brings a pearl into the shop. You know it's the best. It's the one; the perfect pearl. He's asking a high price. A very high price. But no price is too high as far as you are concerned. To own this pearl has been your life's ambition.

And so you sell all the other jewels you own to get enough cash to buy this one, beautiful, flawless, perfect pearl.

You see, said Jesus, there are some things that are worth everything and doing anything to get.

That's what God's kingdom is like. Whether it's treasure hidden in a field or finding a perfect pearl, you go all out to make it yours. You should pull out all the stops to be part of the kingdom of heaven.

Can anything be worth so much to someone?

Is God's kingdom that special?

But what could be more important than heaven itself?

What wouldn't you give for the treasure of being a friend of God for ever?

At least that's what this parable says to me. What about you?

Prayer idea

Digging and searching are the main action words in the two parables.

Invite everyone to mime digging as you pray:

> Lord Jesus, thank you that here at Messy Church we have stumbled across the treasure of knowing you and your love.

Invite everyone to mime searching as you pray:

> Lord Jesus, thank you that here at Messy Church we can find out more and more about the treasure of knowing you and your love.
> Amen

25

Messy words

The parable of the Pharisee and the tax collector

To some who were confident of their own righteousness and looked down on everyone else, Jesus told this parable: 'Two men went up to the temple to pray, one a Pharisee and the other a tax collector. The Pharisee stood by himself and prayed: "God, I thank you that I am not like other people – robbers, evildoers, adulterers – or even like this tax collector. I fast twice a week and give a tenth of all I get."

'But the tax collector stood at a distance. He would not even look up to heaven, but beat his breast and said, "God, have mercy on me, a sinner."

'I tell you that this man, rather than the other, went home justified before God. For all those who exalt themselves will be humbled, and those who humble themselves will be exalted.'

LUKE 18:9–14

Get ready

Just like the other parables in this book, this final one would again have taken people by surprise. It turns normal expectations upside down, just like everything else in the kingdom of God. The Pharisee who knew all about prayer is not put right with God, while the tax collector who in everyone's eyes didn't even deserve to be let into the temple went home justified. It is hard for us, who look back on the story as Christians who know that we are justified by faith and not works, to understand the dismay this story would have caused. Once again the last come first and the first last in the kingdom of heaven.

People were used to seeing members of the Pharisee party at prayer. However, on an earlier occasion in his ministry, Jesus had already criticised them for their many words and their love of being seen to be holy. And elsewhere they had come in for criticism from Jesus for the pernickety way they insisted on keeping every detail of the law (see Matthew 25). No wonder they were so hostile to Jesus. Of course, they sincerely thought they were doing the right thing, just as this Pharisee in his prayer rehearsed the ways in which he had done good things and led a separate holy life. But beware, all of us who believe in God can easily fall into the same trap of spiritual smugness and a judgemental spirit, quick to quote the Bible at people rather than to genuinely listen to them and to love them as God does.

The tax collector was also a familiar sight to Jesus' audience and you can almost hear the hiss of disapproval when Jesus introduces him into the story. These are people who had betrayed their nation by collaborating with the occupying forces and who were responsible for collecting the harsh taxes everyone hated. This prayerful tax collector didn't know where to look, but he knew he had done wrong and felt trapped. No wonder all he can do is cry for mercy. It is a broken heart that God approves of, in contrast to the Pharisee's hard heart that offered no room for God. It is just as is expressed in the Psalms: 'a broken and contrite heart you, God, will not despise' (Psalm 51:17).

According to Luke, this parable is addressed to those who are so full of themselves they don't pray properly. They have all the right words but the wrong attitude. The tax collector in his desperation is in a better place to receive God's forgiveness than the Pharisee. For us too, it is perhaps no bad thing to acknowledge that we so often mess up, because this drives us to turn back to God in true repentance and approach him in a humble way. God welcomes people with messy lives who struggle to find the right words to pray.

Get set

You will need a large, heavy dictionary.

Go!

Thumb through the large dictionary.

Words, words, words.

So many words!

Long words, short words, foreign words, compound words, hard-to-spell words, never-heard-of-before words.

So many words!

In books, emails, texts, tweets, social media posts, newspapers, letters, on the screen, notice boards and advertising boards.

So many words!

We are surrounded by words. Look around where we are at the moment. How many words can you see from where you are sitting?

People say: 'Sticks and stones may break my bones but words can never hurt me.' It's not true. Words can hurt.

Rude words, unkind words, swear words, angry words, empty words, shouted words, put-downs and insults.

Jesus knew all about words. He used words to tell stories. But he knew that words could also be tricky. Particularly the words used in prayers to God.

Some people even think that the more words we use to pray, the more likely God is to hear.

Jesus told a story about prayer once; about words in prayer being used in the temple.

There were two people in the temple congregation who stood out that day.

There was a religious expert. And there was a religious failure.

The religious expert knew all the right words to say.

Lift up your hands dramatically.

He prayed:

Thank you that you made me special and chose me to be faithful.

Thank you that you help me to be holy.

Thank you that I know how to worship you properly.

Thank you that I live life well, keeping feast and fast days and giving my money away.

Thank you that I am not a failure in faith like 'that man over there'.

Pause.

The religious expert used a lot of words.

Not necessarily bad words in themselves but… then 'that man over there' prayed. He was the religious failure.

He didn't really know where to start. He didn't know what to say. He didn't know where to look, but he knew his life was a mess and that he needed help.

All he could pray was: 'Help me, God, my life's a mess.'

Hardly any words at all.

Then Jesus stunned the crowd by saying: Guess which man's prayers were answered?

It was the one who was the religious failure who went home forgiven.

Never? Yes, it's true.

The religious expert knew all the right words, but that's just the point, explained Jesus. They were just words, grand words that may have lifted him up but didn't lift up God.

It was the man with the broken heart whom God could help. The man with all the words had a heart that was too hard for God to help.

Words, words, words.

So many words!

Jesus knew all about which words mattered.

And Jesus should know. Later his followers gave him a sort of nickname. They called Jesus 'the Word'.

He is the only 'word' we need to know.

Prayer idea

Here are just three words that are enough for our prayers. Pray them honestly and regularly from the heart and they will be enough.

Let's learn them:

Sorry
Help
Thanks

Let's use them now with a short space for quiet in between each, talking with and listening to God from our hearts.

Sorry Help Thanks
Amen

Postscript

A parable about Messy Church

[Jesus] also said, 'This is what the kingdom of God is like. A man scatters seed on the ground. Night and day, whether he sleeps or gets up, the seed sprouts and grows, though he does not know how. All by itself the soil produces grain – first the stalk, then the head, then the full kernel in the head. As soon as the grain is ripe, he puts the sickle to it, because the harvest has come.'

MARK 4:26–29

It seems fitting to round off this book of parables for Messy storytellers with a final parable from Jesus. This is one that is unique to Mark's Gospel and, I think, particularly encouraging for us who are engaged in God's mission through Messy Church.

Mark includes it among the other more familiar seed and soil parables covered in this book, and at first glance it seems very similar. Here is a farmer sowing seed that produces a harvest. It is another insight from Jesus into how the kingdom of God works. However, just as with all the other parables, on closer inspection, it takes us by surprise. The farmer's inactivity in the whole process is particularly emphasised. He doesn't water or weed; nor does he protect his crops from the birds. Once he has sown the seed, he does nothing until the harvest time. Is this laziness or does Jesus wants us to understand something more?

The seed, we are told, grows mysteriously 'night and day'. It is something that mostly happens out of sight and, more importantly, out of the control of the farmer. It grows into the harvest 'all by itself'. The Greek word used here is linked to our word 'automatically' and, interestingly, the only other usage of this word in the New Testament is when the gates of the jail opened 'automatically' for Peter in Acts 12:10. In other words, it is all miracle; a miracle from God. No amount of worry or clever planning is required, just faith in God who is at work in people's lives, just as he is in the processes of nature.

This parable is, I believe, especially relevant to us in Messy Church. Journeys to faith can be very long for many of the families with whom we work. The harvest is no overnight miracle but only comes after a long, long time – many years, even. But this parable reminds us that God is definitely at work, even when we can't see much happening; and that there will be a harvest from the sowing one day. We shouldn't get over-anxious, nor become so concerned to see 'fruit' that we are tempted to dig up the still-germinating seed before its time and thereby destroy it. Growing into faith cannot be rushed. We must trust the God of miracles – the God who spoke these words through Isaiah:

> As the heavens are higher than the earth, so are my ways higher than your ways and my thoughts than your thoughts.
> As the rain and the snow come down from heaven and do not return to it without watering the earth and making it bud and flourish, so that it yields seed for the sower and bread for the eater, so is my word that goes out from my mouth: It will not return to me empty, but will accomplish what I desire and achieve the purpose for which I sent it.
> ISAIAH 55:9–11

We cannot hasten God's kingdom into being before its time, nor can we control its progress. This applies in Messy Church as in any other expression of the kingdom on earth. We are called to be patient farmers – even hands-off farmers most of the time – trusting to the Lord of the harvest and rejoicing to observe the slow but sure growth of seed into 'stalk, head and full kernel in the head'. What matters is that we continue to sow and recognise the harvest when it happens. This is definitely not 21st-century business management advice, but it is God's chosen way to bring people home to heaven.

It would be tempting now to go on and suggest a way to tell this parable in a similar style to the others in the book, but I will resist. The truth is that this parable is already being told, again and again, across the world through Messy Church, including in your own Messy Church, if you as a reader are part of a Messy Church team. Messy Church and its miracle growth over recent years; Messy Church and its slow-burn discipleship; Messy Church and its quirky attendance patterns and inevitable fragility; Messy Church with its unpredictable twists and turns; this very sort of Messy Church is perfectly described by this parable. This parable is being retold and relived today, and this should be an encouragement for us all.

Index of Bible verses

Parable references marked in bold.

In *Messy Togetherness,* Martyn Payne looks at Messy Church as an all-age expression of church and the benefits of this to the church community. He explores current thinking about faith development, gives a biblical rationale for the all-age approach, offers practical advice, and shares stories and ideas from across the Messy Church network. This book contains three complete outlines for Messy Church sessions (from the Old Testament, the Gospels and the Epistles), which offer Bible stories with insights into what it means to be intergenerational as church.

Messy Togetherness
Being intergenerational in Messy Church
Martyn Payne

978 0 85746 461 3 £8.99

brfonline.org.uk

Transforming
lives and communities

Christian growth and understanding of the Bible

Resourcing individuals, groups and leaders in churches for their own spiritual journey and for their ministry

Church outreach in the local community

Offering three programmes that churches are embracing to great effect as they seek to engage with their local communities and transform lives

Teaching Christianity in primary schools

Working with children and teachers to explore Christianity creatively and confidently

Children's and family ministry

Working with churches and families to explore Christianity creatively and bring the Bible alive

Visit **brf.org.uk** for more information on BRF's work

brf.org.uk

The Bible Reading Fellowship (BRF) is a Registered Charity (No. 233280)